The CORBA standard provides a quic .... *patn to three-tier architecture. MICO is among the best ORBs for complying to the CORBA standard, thereby reducing the reliance on proprietary initiatives. This factor coupled with the extremely low cost (free) made MICO the standout choice when selecting an ORB for our three-tier architecture initiatives.*

—Michael J. Clark
Software Development Manager
National Access Control, National Digital Television Center
AT&T Broadband & Internet Services

We used MICO as the foundation for building a minimal CORBA for the Palm Pilot architecture. MICO's strongly modular approach gave us a giant leg up and its user community's support was an important added bonus.

—Andreas Paepcke
Senior Research Scientist

MICO has demonstrated to The Open Group that they have a high-quality implementation of the CORBA standards. They should be praised for committing themselves to providing that quality—and for the simple explanation of the technology—into the future.

—Howard Greenwell
Director of Business Development
The Open Group

About the Authors

Arno Puder received his master's degree in computer science from the University of Kaiserslautern and his Ph.D. from the University of Frankfurt. He is working for the Deutsche Telekom AG in CORBA-related projects. His special interests include distributed systems and ubiquitous computing environments.

Kay Römer received his master's degree in computer science from the University of Frankfurt/Main and is currently a Ph.D. student at the ETH Zurich (Switzerland). He is especially interested in distributed systems and operating systems. Besides his studies, he has been involved in projects in the fields of operating systems, distributed systems, graphical windowing systems, and computer graphics.

MICO

An Open Source CORBA Implementation

Third Edition

MICO

An Open Source CORBA Implementation

Third Edition

Arno Puder & Kay Römer

MORGAN KAUFMANN PUBLISHERS

AN IMPRINT OF ACADEMIC PRESS

A Harcourt Science and Technology Company

SAN FRANCISCO   SAN DIEGO   NEW YORK   BOSTON
LONDON   SYDNEY   TOKYO

dpunkt
Verlag für digitale Technologie GmbH
Heidelberg

Copublished by Morgan Kaufmann Publishers and dpunkt.verlag

Morgan Kaufmann Publishers		**dpunkt.verlag**	
Acquisitions Editor	Tim Cox	Senior Editor	Christa Preisendanz
Director of Production & Manufacturing	Yonie Overton		
Production Editors	Heather Collins/Edward Wade		
Editorial Assistant	Brenda Modliszewski		
Cover Design	Ross Carron Design		
Cover Image	Arnold Kaplan/Photonica		
Copyeditor	Jennifer McClain		
Proofreader	Ken DellaPenta		
Printer	Courier Corporation		

This book has been author typeset using LaTeX

Designations used by companies to distinguish their products are often claimed as trademarks or registered trademarks. In all instances where Morgan Kaufmann Publishers is aware of a claim, the product names appear in initial capital or all capital letters. Readers, however, should contact the appropriate companies for more complete information regarding trademarks and registration.

ACADEMIC PRESS
A Harcourt Science and Technology Company
525 B Street, Suite 1900, San Diego, CA 92101-4495, USA
http://www.academicpress.com

Academic Press
Harcourt Place, 32 Jamestown Road, London NW1 7BY, United Kingdom
http://www.hbuk.co.uk/ap/

Morgan Kaufmann Publishers
340 Pine Street, Sixth Floor, San Francisco, CA 94104-3205, USA
http://www.mkp.com

Available in Germany, Austria, and Switzerland from
dpunkt—Verlag für digitale Technologie GmbH
hallo@dpunkt.de
http://www.dpunkt.de

Library of Congress Cataloging-in-Publication Data

Puder, Arno
    MICO : an open source CORBA implementation / Arno Puder & Kay Römer.—3rd ed.
      p. cm.
    Includes bibliographical references and index.
    ISBN 1-55860-666-1
    1. Object-oriented programming (Computer science) 2. CORBA (Computer architecture) I. Römer, Kay. II. Title.
    QA76.64.P83 2000
    005.2′76—dc21   99-086924

MKP ISBN: 1-55860-666-1
dpunkt ISBN: 3-932588-72-X

This book is printed on acid-free paper.

Foreword

During the first year of its existence, the few dozen forward-looking members of the nascent Object Management Group (OMG) spent hours and days trying to define the term "open." Object technology was an easier definition.

I, among the OMG's founding staff and members, knew that object technology would be a good choice for solving the sort of enterprise-wide systems integration problems that crop up everywhere in the computing milieux. We took it for granted that there would never be only a single operating system, single instruction set architecture, single network protocol or topology, and certainly never only one programming language, since different problems call for different solutions. We did understand that a single framework for encapsulating code and data behind a polymorphic interface within an inheritance hierarchy—an object-oriented solution—would better model the muddle of equipment and software that enterprise architects find themselves in.

No, there was scant argument about object technology (though it was hardly mainstream in 1989). There was, however, a continuous argument about the word "open." Over the first two years of OMG's existence, the gradual consensus became something like "a specification arrived at through a democratic, observable, documented process carried out by a neutral organization." This became the hallmark of OMG, and we have leveraged that process over the years to define specifications for everything from systems analysis and design and middleware/application servers to vertical market specifications from air traffic control and manufacturing to life sciences and healthcare systems.

Over this same decade, another kind of "open" has taken hold of the imagination of the computing industry. This is the "open source" movement to provide high-quality, commercial-grade software through freely available implementations shared by developers. Since there is plenty of information about the open-source movement elsewhere (for example, in this book), I will not delve into a definition. Suffice it to say that you can now build high-quality, mission-critical systems from component software parts available for no cost.

In the last two years especially, these two definitions of "open" have collided. Surprisingly, what has happened is that openly derived specifications (such as OMG's) have begun to appear in open-source form (available under license, but without charge). I certainly believed that the interplay between "open source" and "open specification" would flow the other way, but the end result is the same in either case: developers, integrators, and users all have the opportunity to have an impact on specifications and implementations.

This great convergence between two important "open" markets leads us to the book in your hands. While there are at least a dozen open-source implementations of OMG's open CORBA specification, MICO is the only one I know of that was written specifically as a didactic tool. By focusing their efforts in the construction of MICO toward fielding an important book about distributed systems, Puder and Römer have achieved a landmark proof of the value of open-specification, open-source systems. The existence of commercial products based on the MICO CORBA implementation prove their work; this book proves their knowledge. You will find both of immense value in the tough job of building scalable, distributed, heterogeneous systems.

Richard Mark Soley, Ph.D.
Chairman and CEO
Object Management Group, Inc.
December 1999

Foreword to Previous Editions

You are about to start an exciting journey through CORBAland. No, not just the usual textbook trip—this time you can embark on a real hands-on expedition!

The expedition vehicle you will be riding in is called MICO. It is relatively new, but has already attracted a lot of attention and applause. But don't worry: although the terrain may be a bit rough sometimes, this tour book and the enclosed software will help you make it safely through the land of interacting distributed objects.

Luckily, your tour guides, Kay Römer and Arno Puder, are the mechanics who designed and built MICO. I have known the two for a long time and, believe me, you can trust them. I don't know any better guides for practical CORBAland expeditions. In your tour pack you will find the complete specifications and blueprints for the MICO vehicle. These might come in handy in certain situations.

Surely, the trip will be rewarding in many ways. While you follow the tour you will experience for yourself what CORBA is all about:

❏   how CORBA can help you to build distributed applications,

❏   how CORBA works inside, and

❏   how CORBA achieves interoperability.

This journey enters a territory that is still not completely known. You may even discover unsolved problems and challenges to explore for yourself. Please share your views and experiences with other travelers via the MICO discussion forum.

It's time to fasten your seat belts. Enjoy the trip!

Kurt Geihs
University of Frankfurt

Contents

Figures

Preface

A Brief History of MICO

The idea that sparked MICO was to write a new textbook on distributed systems. But not "yet another distributed system textbook" (YADST) merely describing transparency issues and failure semantics. We wanted to write a textbook in the same spirit as Andrew Tanenbaum's famous book on operating systems (see [12]). Tanenbaum chose a pragmatic approach, whereby he first implemented an operating system (namely, MINIX, which stands for Mini Unix) and then wrote the textbook around this implementation.

Our quest was to do something similar for distributed systems. This has the advantage that not only the abstract concepts of distributed systems are explained, but also it is shown how to translate these concepts into "lines of code." For this we first had to decide what to implement. We quickly chose to go for a middleware based on the popular CORBA standard (see [6]). As a tribute to Tanenbaum, we decided back then to call it MICO (which initially stood for Mini CORBA).

We have come a long way since. Two things Tanenbaum did not have during his time when he wrote MINIX: the World Wide Web and a strong open source movement. We saw no harm in releasing the source code of MICO on the Web. After all, we did not have any commercial interest in MICO itself, only in the textbook. It also seemed fashionable for us to release the sources under the GNU General Public License, although neither of us spent a great deal of time to understand its true spirit.

The first public release of MICO was in April 1997. What we did not anticipate was the steadily growing user base who kept us quite busy with bug fixes and new features. Eventually came a time when MICO was no longer "mini," but rather a fully compliant version of the CORBA specification. It had grown beyond what we initially intended. As a consequence we decided to rename MICO, which now stands for MICO Is CORBA (this recursive definition was inspired by GNU, which stands for GNU's Not Unix).

Nowadays MICO is used in both academic as well as commercial environments. Students use it to understand the architecture of a middleware platform. Companies use it because they want to get around the often expensive licensing fees of commercial CORBA implementations. MICO has been branded by The Open Group as CORBA compliant, which demonstrates again that open source can produce industrial-strength software.

This book is a consequence of the success we had with MICO. It complements the forthcoming textbook on distributed systems by giving you something which focuses on MICO from the application programmer's point of view. The software of MICO is and always will be available for free on the Web. This book as well as the accompanying CD with the precompiled binaries adds to the value of the free software, giving you a comprehensive documentation of MICO from an application programmer's point of view.

Working on an open source project is very rewarding. To see MICO being used in various places and to receive support from otherwise strangers is a thrilling experience. Countless programmers from all over the world have made contributions, from small bug fixes to major components. MICO long since has become a community project. Open source is finding its righteous place among commercial software development. MICO is no exception and will certainly continue to grow.

Acknowledgments

A project like MICO is not possible without the help of many people. First, and foremost, we would like to thank all users of MICO who have helped improve its quality through their feedback. Some users of MICO have actively supported us during the development. We would like to thank Christian Becker, Christoph Best, Massimo Di Giorgio, Lars Doelle, Ben Eng, Wil Evers, Karel Gardas, Leif

Jacobsmeier, Elliot Lee, Andrew Metcalfe, Marcus Müller, Martin Sander, Kai-Uwe Sattler, Andreas Schultz, Owen Taylor, Jacques Tremblay, Torben Weis, and Carsten Zerbst for their help and especially the code they contributed. Special thanks go to Frank Pilhofer, who implemented the Portable Object Adapter and who also contributed the documentation in Section 4.4.

The research group Verteilte Systeme und Betriebssysteme (VSB) at the University of Frankfurt, the International Computer Science Institute (ICSI) in Berkeley, and the Distributed Systems group at ETH Zurich provided us with the necessary computing resources and the opportunity to put MICO on the Web. We are thankful for their support.

Finally, we would like to thank our publishers, Christa Preisendanz from dpunkt.verlag and Tim Cox from Morgan Kaufmann Publishers, for their invaluable support. Without them, the MICO distribution would not have been possible.

1 Introduction

1.1 What Is MICO?

The acronym MICO expands to **MICO Is CORBA**. For a more elaborate answer, we first need to explain the term *CORBA*. COR-BA stands for *Common Object Request Broker Architecture*, and it describes the architecture of a middleware platform that supports the implementation of applications in distributed and heterogeneous environments (see [6]). The CORBA standard is issued by the Object Management Group (OMG), an international organization with over 800 information software vendors, software developers, and users. The goal of the OMG is the establishment of industry guidelines and object management specifications to provide a common framework for application development.

One important aspect of CORBA is that it is a *specification* and not an *implementation*. CORBA provides a framework allowing applications to interoperate in a distributed and heterogeneous environment, but it does not prescribe any specific technology for how to implement the CORBA standard. The standard is freely available via the World Wide Web at *www.omg.org*. Currently, there exist many implementations of CORBA focusing on different market segments.

CORBA has gained much attention and is being used for many different projects, which is reflected by the steady growth of literature on the subject. All these books have a major drawback, however: they assume that you have access to a CORBA implementation to try it out yourself. There are many commercially available CORBA products, such as Orbix from Iona or VisiBroker from Inprise. But you have to pay a lot of money if you wish to buy a license.

This is where MICO comes in. MICO is a freely available and complete CORBA-compliant implementation. What you are holding in your hands right now is enough for you to play with CORBA without paying big fees in advance. The CD with this book contains the complete source code of MICO as well as precompiled binaries for various platforms. MICO has become quite popular as an open source project and is widely used for different purposes. As a major milestone, MICO has been branded as CORBA compliant by The Open Group, thus demonstrating that open source can indeed produce industrial-strength software. Our goal is to keep MICO compliant with the latest CORBA standard. The sources of MICO are placed under the GNU copyright notice (see Chapter 9). The following design principles guided the implementation of MICO:

MICO's design principles

1. Start from scratch: use only what standard Unix API has to offer; don't rely on proprietary or specialized libraries.

2. Use C++ for the implementation.

3. Make use of only widely available, nonproprietary tools.

4. Omit "bells and whistles": implement only what is required for a CORBA-compliant implementation.

5. Clear design even for implementation internals to ensure extensibility.

MICO is a fully compliant CORBA implementation (it is actually worthwhile to look up the definition of "CORBA compliant" in section [0.5] of the CORBA standard; some CORBA implementations, including commercial ones, did not pay too much attention to this definition). The following is a (nonexhaustive) list of features that you will find in the current version of MICO contained on the CD accompanying this distribution:

❏ IDL to C++ mapping

❏ full support for dynamic programming: Dynamic Invocation Interface (DII), Dynamic Skeleton Interface (DSI), Interface Repository (IR), Dynamic **Any**

❏ Portable Object Adapter (POA)

❏ Value Type Semantics

❏ Internet Inter-ORB Protocol (IIOP) as native protocol

❏ IIOP over SSL

❏ modular ORB design: new transport protocols and object adapters can easily be attached to the ORB, even at runtime using loadable modules

❏ support for nested method invocations

❏ interceptors

❏ **Any** offers an interface for inserting and extracting constructed types that were not known at compile time

❏ **Any** and **TypeCode** support recursive subtyping as defined by the RM-ODP

❏ full BOA implementation, including all activation modes, support for object migration, object persistence, and the implementation repository

❏ BOA can load object implementations into clients at runtime using loadable modules

❏ support for using MICO from within X11 applications (Xt, Gtk, Tcl, and Qt)

❏ interoperable naming, event, property, relationship, time, and trading services compliant with the Common Object Services Specification (COSS)

❏ graphical Interface Repository browser that allows you to invoke arbitrary methods on arbitrary interfaces

Features implemented in MICO

Most of the features are required for a compliant implementation of the CORBA standard (like the DII and the DSI). Surprisingly enough, many commercial "compliant" CORBA implementations are missing some of these features! The current version of MICO supports only the IDL to C++ mapping. But using MICO's IIOP implementation already gives you access to CORBA objects written in Java (this is described in detail in Chapter 6).

1.2 Supported Platforms

MICO supports GNU

MICO can be built using GNU tools, and it should be possible to port MICO to platforms where the GNU tools are available. The CD that accompanies this book contains the binaries for the following platforms:

❏ Solaris 2.6 on Sun SPARC

❏ AIX 4.2 on IBM RS/6000

❏ Linux 2.2.x on Intel x86

❏ Digital Unix 4.x on DEC Alpha (no exceptions)

❏ HP-UX 10.20 on PA-RISC

❏ Windows NT and 95

1.3 Problems or Questions?

Many people have used MICO and helped make it what it is today. Some companies are even using it for commercial purposes, which is not ruled out by the GNU General Public License. Although some people think MICO is quite competitive with commercially available CORBA implementations costing thousands of dollars, you should keep in mind that MICO is not a product. The money you have spent is for the book and the CD containing this distribution, not for MICO itself. Although we will maintain and release new versions of MICO, we cannot offer the same customer support as other companies.

We have set up a mailing list where many users of MICO around the world have already subscribed. If you encounter problems or if you have questions regarding MICO, you can subscribe to this mailing list. We will do our best to answer your questions. The mailing list provides a forum where MICO users contribute with their experience to help each other solve problems. Please visit MICO's home page for instructions on how to subscribe to the mailing list.

Mailing list

Although the current version of MICO is quite stable, you should visit our home page frequently for updates. We will continue to develop MICO, providing bug fixes as well as new features. Information about the MICO project is available at *www.mico.org*.

Online information

1.4 Overview of This Book

This book is a combination of an installation guide, tutorial, user, and reference manual. Here is a chapter-by-chapter overview of the book:

Chapter 2: Before you can get going using MICO, you need to install it on your system. The CD that accompanies this book contains precompiled binaries as well as the complete sources for MICO. This chapter describes how to install MICO on your system.

Chapter 3: Here we provide a guided tour through MICO and explain the basics of CORBA as well as how to use MICO for a simple client/server application. We demonstrate how to turn a simple, one-address-space application written in C++ into a distributed application running on different hosts using MICO.

Chapter 4: MICO comes with a whole set of different tools, which are described in this chapter. The simple programming example from Chapter 3 is used in more and more complex scenarios to show things like the usage of CORBA's activation modes or how to migrate objects between hosts.

Chapter 5: MICO implements the IDL to C++ mapping as defined in the CORBA standard. This chapter contains some useful information that might make your life a bit easier. It also describes some design issues specific to MICO.

Chapter 6: We have implemented IIOP to allow interoperability with other ORB implementations. In this chapter, we demonstrate how to make MICO interoperate with Orbix and VisiBroker.

Chapter 7: MICO is shipped with a CORBA-compliant naming service as defined in COSS. In this chapter, we describe how you can use the naming service for your applications.

Chapter 8: As a little add-on, we have implemented a graphical browser for the IR as well as a generic user interface for the DII. This chapter tells you how to use it.

Chapter 9: The last chapter contains the GNU Library General Public License as well as the GNU General Public License under which MICO is placed. If you are considering using MICO for more than just learning about CORBA, you are advised to read it.

How to read this book

This book is not meant to be read from first to last page. Chapter 2 is mandatory since you must first install MICO before you can use it. The tutorial provided in Chapter 3 gives you a taste of some features of MICO. Even for CORBA gurus it would be beneficial to read this chapter completely. The remainder of the book should be consulted as you get more into the details of CORBA. Use the table of contents and the index to look up relevant topics.

This book does not explain what CORBA is and what it can be used for. We do not want to compete with all the textbooks about CORBA. Instead, we hope this book serves as a complement to your favorite CORBA textbook, one that allows you to find out for yourself what CORBA is all about. We have included ported versions of various sample applications that are shipped with other CORBA textbooks. See Appendix A for more details.

MICO version

Throughout this book, the version of MICO on the CD is referred to as <version>. When used as part of a command, you have to replace **version** with the actual version number, which

can be found in a file called `VERSION` located in the root directory
of the CD. The version number consists of three digits separated
by dots. The first two digits indicate the version number of the
CORBA standard that MICO implements.

2 Installation

This chapter gives a detailed description of how to install MICO on your system. There are basically three possibilities: you can run MICO directly from the CD (described in Section 2.2), you can install precompiled MICO binaries on your hard disk (described in Section 2.3), or you can compile MICO yourself (described in Section 2.4 for Unix and Section 2.5 for Windows). Read this chapter carefully before trying to install MICO.

2.1 Prerequisites

Before you try anything with MICO, you should make sure that your system provides the prerequisites listed in this section. There are three different kinds of prerequisites, depending on what you want to do:

1. Compiling MICO applications. This is mandatory for all users of MICO. If your system does not meet these minimal prerequisites, you will not be able to do anything with MICO at all. See Section 2.1.1 for details.

   Compiling MICO applications

2. Compiling MICO. If the binaries contained on the CD do not match with your system, you may need to compile and install MICO from the source distribution. Before you try to compile the MICO sources, you should make sure that the tools listed in Section 2.1.2 are properly installed on your system.

   Compiling MICO

3. Compiling the Interface Repository (IR) browser. The IR browser is not required if you want to compile MICO applications. If you managed to install the binaries contained on

   Compiling the IR browser

the CD, you will already have a working version of the IR browser. If you need to compile the IR browser yourself, you have to make sure that your system provides the prerequisites listed in Section 2.1.3.

2.1.1 Compiling MICO applications

In order to compile your own MICO applications, you need a C++ compiler and associated C++ libraries. MICO supports a wide variety of C++ compilers. Besides the various GNU compilers, some commercial products are supported as well:

- ❑ gcc 2.95 (`tools/gcc-2.95.2.tar.gz` on CD)

- ❑ egcs 1.1.x

- ❑ egcs 1.0.x

- ❑ HP aC++ A.01.12

- ❑ Sun SPARC Compiler 4.2

- ❑ AIX C++ 3.1.4.6

- ❑ Cygnus CDK Beta 20 (`tools/cdk.exe` on CD)

- ❑ Microsoft Visual C++ 6.0 plus ServicePack 2

Do not mix C++ compilers

During installation, you will be asked which compiler you intend to use. When compiling MICO applications, you have to make sure you use the same compiler you selected during installation. C++ compilers cannot be mixed because they produce incompatible binaries. Even GNU compilers with differing minor version numbers (the number after the first dot) are incompatible. So you have to be very careful, especially if you have installed several GNU compilers on your system. See Appendix B for common problems. You can find out the version number of the GNU compiler you are using by issuing the command `c++ -v`.

egcs is recommended

Furthermore, C++ compilers differ heavily in quality and supported C++ features. The preceding list is ordered by descending quality. Visual C++ from Microsoft is by far the worst compiler. Older GNU C++ versions (2.7.2, 2.8) have major problems on many

platforms and a huge memory footprint. We recommend using egcs
1.1.x or gcc 2.95.1.

If you are running Linux, take care if you have installed Suse   *Linux*
Linux 5.0 or a newer RedHat release. The g++ 2.7.2.1 shipped
with them is broken and cannot compile MICO applications. It
will fail with an `internal compiler error`. In this case, you can
either reinstall g++ from an older release (e.g., Suse Linux 4.4.x)
or you can compile g++ yourself.

There are two major ways to use MICO on top of Windows
NT or 95. The first one is to install Cygnus CDK, a freely avail-   *Windows and CDK*
able version of the GNU tools for Windows. It contains the GNU
compiler, along with the most important Unix command line utili-
ties. The following sections do not contain special notes for Cygnus
CDK because it behaves much like a Unix environment.

Although the CDK is quite stable, it is still in beta testing and   *Problems with*
has some problems: *CDK*

❏ On stand-alone machines that are not connected to a name
    server, resolving IP addresses other than 127.0.0.1 into host
    names will hang forever. This is either a problem with the
    CDK or with Windows in general. On stand-alone machines,
    you therefore have to make all servers bind to 127.0.0.1 by
    specifying `-ORBIIOPAddr inet:127.0.0.1:<port>` on the
    command line.

❏ There seems to be a problem with automatic TCP port num-
    ber selection. Usually, you bind to port number 0 and the
    system automatically picks an unused port for you. This ba-
    sically works with CDK but sometimes causes hanging con-
    nections. The solution is to always explicitly specify port
    numbers, that is, give *all* servers, even ones that are started
    by `micod`, the option `-ORBIIOPAddr inet:<host>:<port>`,
    where `<port>` is nonzero.

To install the CDK, run the setup program `cdk.exe`. Note that
you have to install it in the directory the setup program suggests
(`c:\cygnus`); otherwise, some programs will not be able to find
their configuration files. Then create `c:\bin` and copy `sh.exe` into
it. Likewise, create `c:\lib` and copy `cpp.exe` into it:

```
mkdir c:\bin
mkdir c:\lib
cd c:\cygnus\cygwin-b20\H-i586-cygwin32
copy bin\bash.exe c:\bin\sh.exe
copy lib\gcc-lib\i586-cygwin32\egcs-2.91.57\cpp.exe \
    c:\lib
```

Windows and Visual C++

The second alternative is to use Visual C++ from Microsoft. See Section 2.5.1 for some comments regarding this compiler.

2.1.2   Compiling MICO

If you want to compile MICO yourself on a Unix system, you need the following tool in addition to the C++ compiler: GNU make version 3.7 or newer (`tools/make-3.78.1.tar.gz` on CD). Issue the following command to find out the version of this tool if you have already installed it: `gmake -v`.

2.1.3   Compiling the interface repository browser

If you want to compile the graphical interface repository browser on a Unix system, you will need Sun's Java Developer's Kit (JDK), JavaCUP (a parser generator for Java), flex, and bison:

❑   JDK 1.1.5
    java.sun.com/products/jdk/1.1.5/index.html

❑   JavaCUP 0.10g
    www.cs.princeton.edu/˜appel/modern/java/CUP/

❑   flex 2.5.2 or newer (`tools/flex-2.5.4a.tar.gz` on CD)

❑   bison 1.22 or newer (`tools/bison-1.28.tar.gz` on CD)

For copyright reasons, we cannot put the JDK and JavaCUP on the CD, so you have to get them from the Web.

2.2 Running from CD

2.2.1 Unix

Insert the CD into your drive, become root, and mount the CD
to somewhere in your file system (e.g., `/tmp/mnt`). On Linux, you
have to issue the following commands for this (similar on other
systems):

```
mkdir /tmp/mnt
su
mount -rt iso9660 /dev/cdrom /tmp/mnt
```

Now you should run the `mount-mico` script to figure out which
binaries to use for your system:

```
/tmp/mnt/unix-bin/mount-mico
```

If the CD does not contain binaries for your system, the script
will tell you so. In this case, you must compile MICO yourself (see
Sections 2.4 and 2.5 for details). Otherwise, the script will create
two shell scripts in your home directory. Execute one of them to
set up environment variables for MICO:

```
# in csh or tcsh
source $HOME/mico-setup.csh

# in sh, ksh, ash, bash, or zsh
. $HOME/mico-setup.sh
```

2.2.2 Windows

Under Windows, the CD is mapped to a logical device. Assuming
that the CD is mapped to logical device F:, the binaries for Windows using Visual C++ are located in `F:\win32-bin`. All you need
to do is to set the environment variable `PATH` to include this path:

```
PATH F:\win32-bin;%PATH%
```

2.3   Installing from CD

2.3.1   Unix

Insert the CD into your drive, become root, and mount the CD to somewhere in your file system (e.g., /tmp/mnt). On Linux, you have to issue the following commands for this (similar on other systems):

```
mkdir /tmp/mnt
su
mount -rt iso9660 /dev/cdrom /tmp/mnt
```

Now you can run the install script, which will ask you some questions and will install MICO:

```
/tmp/mnt/unix-bin/install-mico
```

If there are no binaries for your system on the CD, the script will try to compile MICO for your system. This will only work if you have installed the tools, as explained in Section 2.1. Before using MICO, you must execute a shell script to set up some environment variables (supposing you installed into /usr/local/mico):

```
# in csh or tcsh
source /usr/local/mico/lib/mico-setup.csh

# in sh, ksh, ash, bash, or zsh
. /usr/local/mico/lib/mico-setup.sh
```

To automate this, you can include the appropriate command into your .cshrc or .profile files.

2.3.2   Windows

Under Windows, the CD is mapped to a logical device. Assuming that the CD is mapped to logical device F:, the binaries for Windows using Visual C++ are located in F:\win32-bin. All you need to do is to copy all the files contained in this directory to the desired location. For example, if you want to copy the binaries to C:\mico, type the following instructions:

```
MKDIR C:\mico
XCOPY /q /s F:\win32-bin\*.* C:\mico
PATH C:\mico;%PATH%
```

2.4   Installing from Sources (Unix)

The MICO sources are shipped as a tarred and gzipped archive on the CD called `mico-<version>.tar.gz`, where `<version>` is the version number of the MICO release contained on the CD. Unpack the archive using the following command:

You can get the latest MICO release from the Web using the URLs given in Section 1.2

```
gzip -dc mico-<version>.tar.gz | tar xf -
```

You are left with a new directory `mico` containing the MICO sources.

To save you the hassle of manually editing `Makefiles` and such, MICO comes with a configuration script that checks your system for required programs and other configuration issues. The script, called `configure`, supports several important command line options:

`--help`
> This option gives an overview of all supported command line options.

`--prefix=<install-directory>`
> With this option, you tell `configure` where the MICO programs and libraries should be installed after compilation. This defaults to `/usr/local`.

`--disable-optimize`
> This disables the `-O` option when compiling C/C++ files.

`--enable-debug`
> This enables the `-g` option when compiling C/C++ files.

`--disable-shared`
> This option builds the MICO library as a static library instead of a shared one. Shared libraries currently work only on ELF-based systems (e.g., Linux, Solaris, Digital Unix,

AIX, and HP-UX). If you do not use the --disable-shared option, either you must make sure the directory where the MICO library resides is by default searched for shared libraries by the dynamic linker (/usr/lib and /lib on most systems) or you must include the directory in the environment variable that tells the dynamic linker where to search for additional shared libraries. This variable is called LIBPATH on AIX, SHLIB_PATH on HP-UX, and LD_LIBRARY_PATH on all the other systems. To run the generated binaries before doing a make install, you have to set this environment variable like this:

```
# AIX
export LIBPATH=<mico-path>/mico/orb:$LIBPATH
# HP-UX
export SHLIB_PATH=<mico-path>/mico/orb:\
  $SHLIB_PATH
# others
export LD_LIBRARY_PATH=<mico-path>/mico/orb:\
  $LD_LIBRARY_PATH
```

where <mico-path> is the absolute path of the directory the MICO sources were unpacked in.

--disable-dynamic

This option disables dynamic loading of CORBA objects into a running executable. For dynamic loading to work, your system must support either dlopen() and friends or shl_load() and friends (see Section 4.3.4 for details).

--enable-final

This builds a size-optimized version of the MICO library. It will need lots of memory during compilation but will considerably reduce the size of the resulting library.

--disable-mini-stl

MICO makes use of the Standard Template Library (STL). For environments that do not provide an STL implementation, MICO comes with its own slim STL (called MiniSTL), which is simply a subset of the standard STL sufficient to compile MICO. By default, MICO will use MiniSTL. If you want to use the system-supplied STL for some reason, use the option `--disable-mini-stl`. MiniSTL works well with g++ and greatly reduces compilation time and the size of the binaries.

`--disable-except`

This disables exception handling. On some platforms (e.g., DEC Alpha), g++ has very buggy exception-handling support that inhibits the compilation of MICO with exception handling enabled. If this happens, try turning off exception handling using this option.

`--disable-namespace`

This option maps IDL modules to C++ nested classes. By default, modules are mapped to C++ namespaces.

`--with-qt=<qt-path>`

This enables support for Qt. `<qt-path>` is the directory in which Qt has been installed.

`--with-gtk=<gtk-path>`

This enables support for Gtk. `<gtk-path>` is the directory in which Gtk has been installed.

`--with-tcl=<tcl-path>`

This enables support for Tcl. `<tcl-path>` is the directory in which Tcl has been installed.

`--with-ssl=<SSLeay-path>`

This enables support for SSL. `<SSLeay-path>` is the directory in which SSLeay has been installed.

Now you should run `configure` with the command line options you need, for example:

```
cd mico
./configure --with-qt=/usr/local/qt
```

Use `gmake` to start compilation and install the programs and libraries, possibly becoming root before installation:

```
gmake
gmake install
```

On some systems, you have to take special actions after installing a shared library to tell the dynamic linker about the new library. For instance, on Linux you have to run `ldconfig` as root:

```
/sbin/ldconfig -v
```

2.5   Installing from Sources (Windows)

Installing MICO under Windows using the Visual C++ compiler is sufficiently different to warrant its own section. Beware that this compiler is not among the most technically solid pieces of engineering. Make sure you have applied all available Service Packs (Microsoft terminology for bug fixes). It is also advisable to check the latest release notes for MICO on the Windows platform, which are contained in the file `README-WIN32`.

See file `README-WIN32` *for further comments regarding VC++*

2.5.1   Prerequisites

You will need Visual C++ 5.0 Service Pack 3 or (preferred) Visual C++ 6.0 Service Pack 2 to compile MICO for Windows. Note that without installing appropriate service packs for Visual C++, you will not be able to compile the sources or write MICO applications. Windows versions of flex and bison are not required. The MICO distribution already contains the files generated by these tools. VC++ 5.0 SP3 is available from *www.microsoft.com/msdownload/ vs97sp/full.asp*. VC++ 6.0 Service Packs are available at *msdn. microsoft.com/vstudio/sp/default.asp*.

Bug fixes for VC++

The Windows 95 implementation of the TCP/IP protocol stack causes problems with MICO applications. You need to download and install the WinSock2 library, which fixes these problems. You can download WinSock2 from the Microsoft Web server for free: *www.microsoft.com/windows95/downloads/contents/ wuadmintools/s_wunetworkingtools/w95sockets2/default.asp?site= 95*.

Problems with TCP under Windows 95

IMPORTANT: You also need to make sure that the environment variables are set properly for Visual C++. There is a batch file called `VCVARS32.bat` specifically for this purpose. Be sure to run this batch file, which is part of VC++, before you try to compile MICO.

Once you have made sure that your Windows platform meets all the above-mentioned prerequisites, you can unpack the MICO sources. The sources are shipped as a zipped archive on the CD called `mico-<version>.zip`, where `<version>` is the version number of the MICO release contained on the CD. Unpack the archive at the desired location.

2.5.2   Compiling the MICO sources

Change to the directory where you have unzipped the MICO sources and edit the file `MakeVars.win32`. Set the `SRCDIR` variable to the location of the MICO directory (no trailing backslash). There is no need to run a `configure` script since MICO is preconfigured for Windows.

VC++ comes with its own Makefile tool called `nmake`. Unfortunately, this tool is sufficiently incompatible with other make tools. For this reason, the MICO distribution contains a second set of Makefiles. These Makefiles have the suffix `.win32` and are tailored to work with `nmake`. To compile MICO on your system, type the following in the MICO top-level directory:

```
nmake /f Makefile.win32
```

If you are running Windows 95/98, the command line shell suffers from some serious deficiencies. On those platforms, you need to invoke the compilation process using the following command instead:

```
nmake /f Makefile.win32 w95-all
```

The make process will build all the necessary DLLs and executables in a subdirectory called `win32-bin`, which will be created during compilation. The content of this directory is the only thing you need for building MICO applications. You can move it to your preferred location. The build will require around 300MB (the demo directory another 90MB).

You should modify the PATH environment variable to include this directory. If, for example, the MICO sources were unzipped in C:\mico, type the following:

```
PATH C:\mico\win32-bin;%PATH%
```

2.5.3   Writing MICO applications using the IDE

IDE's project files are functionally similar to Makefiles

All the examples that come with MICO depend on Makefiles for the building process. The advantage of a tool like Visual C++ is that it offers an *Integrated Development Environment* (IDE), which combines editor, compiler, and debugger in one tool. The IDE also manages all the files that belong to a project. This section gives you an indication of how to use the IDE together with MICO. First, you have to tell Visual C++ where MICO is located. You do this in the *Tools/Options* dialog, in the *Directories* tab, adding the following directories to *Include path* (assuming MICO was installed under c:\mico):

```
C:\mico\win32-bin\include\windows
C:\mico\win32-bin\include
```

These lines have to be first in the list (use the move buttons to move them to the first position). Next, add the following path to *Library path*

```
C:\mico\win32-bin\lib
```

and to the *Executables path* accordingly

```
C:\mico\win32-bin
```

In the project settings, make the following changes:

Compiler: Define _WINDOWS in the *Preprocessor* options. In the *Code Generation* options, use the multithreaded DLL version of the runtime library because that's the way MICO was compiled.

Linker: Add micoXXX.lib and wsock32.lib (where XXX is the three-digit version number of MICO without the dots) to the

Object/Library modules input field. Before you do this, select *All configurations* in the upper left combo box named *Settings for* so that the settings will apply to both release and debug builds.

Additionally, you can integrate your IDL files in the build process so that the IDE notices any changes made to them and recompiles the IDL specifications when necessary. First, add the IDL file to your project, then go to *Project/Settings* and select this file, or right-click on the IDL file and choose *Settings*, select the *Custom Build* tab, and enter

```
idl --c++-suffix=cpp [other options] $(InputPath)
```

into the *Build Command* list box. In the *Output* files list box, enter

```
$(InputName).h
$(InputName).cpp
```

For inserting `$(..)`, you can also use the pop-up buttons at the bottom of the dialog, or you can use the real filename instead. The output files of the IDL compiler are created in the current directory, normally the root of the project. If the output filename is `foo.cpp`, you have to add `foo.cpp` to the project. This can be done even before the file exists, by entering it into the file dialog.

2.6 Road Map

The CD contains the following files and directories:

`VERSION`	contains MICO version number
`mico-<version>.tar.gz`	tarred and gzipped MICO sources
`mico-<version>.zip`	zipped MICO sources
`src`	unpacked MICO sources
`unix-bin`	binaries for various Unix systems
`win32-bin`	binaries for Windows 95/NT
`tools`	some GNU tools needed for using and compiling MICO
`contrib`	useful third-party software that uses MICO

The `unix-bin` directory contains some shell scripts that are of importance for you:

`mico-install`	install MICO binaries from CD
`mico-mount`	prepare running MICO binaries from CD

The `src` directory contains the following subdirectories:

`admin`	scripts and programs needed to build MICO
`auxdir`	ORB-related stuff (dispatchers for various GUI environments; `libmicoaux` is built in this directory)
`coss`	CORBA services (`libmicocoss` is built in this directory)
`daemon`	Object Adapter daemon (`micod`)
`demo`	some examples
`doc`	documentation
`idl`	IDL compiler (`idl`)
`imr`	implementation repository and administration tool
`include`	C++ and IDL include files
`ir`	interface repository and IR server (`ird`)
`man`	manual pages
`orb`	ORB core (`libmico` is built here)
`test`	some test cases to check the ORB and IDL compiler
`tools`	miscellaneous tool programs, at present only the IR browser and IOR dumper

3 CORBA Tutorial Using MICO

This chapter presents a guided tour through MICO to get you going with your first MICO application. We assume you have successfully installed MICO on your system and are now eager to write your first program. Some C++ knowledge is required to understand the programs. In Section 3.1, we describe part of the rationale behind CORBA, and in Section 3.2 we briefly describe some of the terminology used in CORBA. This should give you a rough idea of what CORBA is all about. Note that this description does not explain everything there is to know about CORBA.

The various subsections of Section 3.3 give you a hands-on example of how to use MICO for a simple client/server application. It is probably a good idea to go successively through all examples. In Section 3.3.1, we present a stand-alone C++ program that does not use MICO at all. In Section 3.3.2, we rewrite the application using MICO for the communication between the client and the server side. In this second stage of our tutorial, the complete application still runs in one address space. Finally, in Section 3.3.3, we show how to separate the client from the server and make them run in different address spaces or even on different hosts using the network for communication.

3.1 Objects in Distributed Systems

Modern programming languages employ the *object paradigm* to structure computation within a single operating system process. The next logical step is to distribute a computation over multiple processes on a single machine or even on different machines. Because object orientation has proven to be an adequate means for developing and maintaining large-scale applications, it seems

Object paradigm is used to structure applications in heterogeneous distributed environments

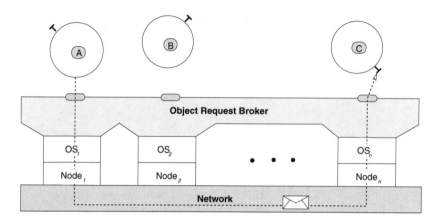

reasonable to apply the object paradigm to distributed computation as well: objects are distributed over the machines within a networked environment and communicate with each other.

As a fact of life, the computers within a networked environment differ in hardware architecture, operating system software, and the programming languages used to implement the objects. That is what we call a *heterogeneous distributed environment*. To allow communication between objects in such an environment, you need a rather complex piece of software called a *middleware platform*. The term *middleware* derives from the fact that it is a piece of software that resides between the application and the operating system. Think of it as a tablecloth that spreads out over the network, trying to hide some of the underlying complexities and offering the same Application Programming Interface (API) at each node of the network. Figure 3.1 illustrates the role of a middleware platform within a heterogeneous distributed environment.

The Common Object Request Broker Architecture (CORBA) is a specification of such a middleware platform by the Object Management Group (OMG) (see [6]). MICO provides a full CORBA 2.3 compliant implementation. CORBA 2.3 addresses the following issues:

Object orientation: Objects are the basic building blocks of CORBA applications.

Distribution transparency: A caller uses the same mechanisms to invoke an object, whether it is located in the same address space, on the same machine, or on a remote machine.

Hardware, operating system, and language independence: CORBA components can be implemented using different programming languages on different hardware architectures running different operating systems.

Vendor independence: CORBA-compliant implementations from different vendors interoperate.

CORBA is an open standard in the sense that anybody can obtain the specification and implement it, as we did. Besides its technical features, this is considered one of CORBA's main advantages over other proprietary solutions.

3.2 Overview of CORBA

This section presents a short overview of CORBA. As mentioned before, this book does not claim to be a thorough introduction to CORBA. Some familiarity with CORBA is assumed, and this section should be seen only as a brief overview of the nuts and bolts of CORBA. Figure 3.2 depicts the basic components of a CORBA platform. All CORBA components are depicted in gray, whereas the application running on top of it is shown in white.

The central piece of the architecture is the *Object Request Broker* (ORB), which serves as a "software bus" connecting different objects over the network. On the client side, the ORB offers an interface to send an operation invocation, while on the server side the ORB offers an API to deliver an operation invocation to a server. The ORB's task is to locate an appropriate server and to deliver the operation invocation to the server via an *Object Adapter* (OA). The purpose of the OA is to dispatch method invocations to skeletons and support the life cycle of server objects (e.g., creation and deletion of objects). Older versions of the CORBA specification included a *Basic Object Adapter* (BOA), which, as the name implies, was rather simple. It was also not very well specified, which inhibited portability of CORBA applications. As of version 2.2 of the

ORB

BOA and POA

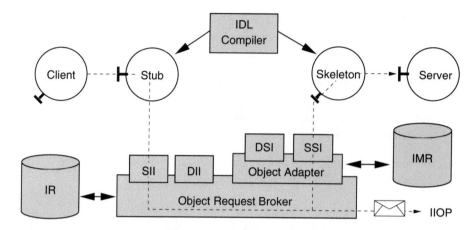

Figure 3.2
Components of a CORBA platform

CORBA standard, the BOA was replaced by the *Portable Object Adapter* (POA). MICO supports both the BOA and the POA.

DII and DSI   At the client side, the ORB offers a generic API, the *Dynamic Invocation Interface* (DII), to send operation invocations. At the server side, the OA delivers an operation invocation via the *Dynamic Skeleton Interface* (DSI), which mirrors the behavior of the DII for the server side. A static interface between a client and a

IDL   server is defined through an *Interface Definition Language* (IDL). Whereas the DII and DSI represent generic interfaces to the ORB and are usually used for bridges, an IDL specification may be used to generate type-safe, application-specific interfaces to the ORB.

SII and SSI   On the client side, the static interface between the client and the ORB is called the *Static Invocation Interface* (SII), and on the server side this interface is called the *Static Skeleton Interface* (SSI). An *IDL compiler* is used to generate a *stub* and a *skeleton* out of an IDL specification. The stub acts as a proxy for the client, whereas the skeleton is responsible for dispatching an operation invocation to an actual implementation of that operation.

IR and IMR   CORBA also defines two runtime databases. The *Interface Repository* (IR) contains IDL specifications that may be queried at runtime. The IR can be used to query details of user-defined IDL types and therefore provides a basic type reflection mechanism. The second database is called the *Implementation Repository*

(IMR), and it contains information regarding details of the servers (i.e., which executable needs to be launched for which servers). The OA requires this information for automatic server activation.

The CORBA standard also includes an inter-ORB protocol called the *Internet Inter-ORB Protocol* (IIOP), which describes the on-the-wire representations of basic and constructed IDL types as well as *Protocol Data Units* (PDUs) needed for the protocol. The design of IIOP was driven by the goal to keep it simple, scalable, and general. IIOP uses TCP/IP for transporting operation invocations and their parameters between different ORBs.

IIOP

3.3 Sample Program

To get you started with MICO, this section presents an example of how to turn a single-process, object-oriented program into a MICO application.

3.3.1 Stand-alone program

Imagine a bank that maintains accounts of its customers. An object implementing such a bank account offers three operations: *deposit* a certain amount of money, *withdraw* a certain amount of money, and *balance*, an operation that returns the current account balance. The state of an account object consists of the current balance. The following C++ code fragment shows the class declaration for such an account object:

Sample program models bank accounts in a client/server scenario

```
1:  class Account {
2:      long _current_balance;
3:  public:
4:      Account();
5:      void deposit( unsigned long amount );
6:      void withdraw( unsigned long amount );
7:      long balance();
8:  };
```

The preceding class declaration describes the *interface* and the *state* of an account object. The actual *implementation*, which reflects the behavior of an account, is shown below:

Server

```
 1:  Account::Account()
 2:  {
 3:      _current_balance = 0;
 4:  }
 5:  void Account::deposit( unsigned long amount )
 6:  {
 7:      _current_balance += amount;
 8:  }
 9:  void Account::withdraw( unsigned long amount )
10:  {
11:      _current_balance -= amount;
12:  }
13:  long Account::balance()
14:  {
15:      return _current_balance;
16:  }
```

Client   Here is a piece of code that makes use of a bank account:

```
 1:  #include <iostream.h>
 2:
 3:  int main( int argc, char *argv[] )
 4:  {
 5:      Account acc;
 6:
 7:      acc.deposit( 700 );
 8:      acc.withdraw( 250 );
 9:      cout << "balance is " << acc.balance() << endl;
10:
11:      return 0;
12:  }
```

Since a new account has an initial balance of 0, the preceding code will print out *"balance is 450."*

3.3.2   MICO application

Now we want to turn the stand-alone implementation from the previous section into a MICO application. Because CORBA objects can be implemented in different programming languages, the specification of an object's *interface* and *implementation* have to be separated. The implementation is done using the selected programming language, but the interface is specified using the Interface Definition Language (IDL). Basically, the CORBA IDL looks like C++ reduced to class and type declarations (i.e., you *cannot* write down the implementation of a class method using IDL). Here is the interface declaration for our account object in CORBA IDL:

IDL is used for the specification of object interfaces

```
1:  interface Account {
2:      void deposit( in unsigned long amount );
3:      void withdraw( in unsigned long amount );
4:      long balance();
5:  };
```

As you can see, it looks quite similar to the class declaration in Section 3.3.1. The `in` declarator declares `amount` as an input parameter to the `deposit()` and `withdraw()` methods. Usually, you would save this declaration to a file called `account.idl`.

The next step is to run this interface declaration through the IDL compiler that will generate code in the selected implementation programming language (C++ in our example). The MICO IDL compiler is called `idl` and is used like this:

```
idl account.idl
```

The IDL compiler will generate two files: `account.h` and `account.cc` (see Figure 3.3). The former contains class declarations for the base class of the account object implementation and the stub class a client will use to invoke methods on remote account objects. The latter contains implementations of those classes and some supporting code. As shown in Figure 3.3, the generated code is compiled and linked with the client and server parts of the application.

For each interface declared in an IDL file, the MICO IDL compiler produces three C++ classes. Note that C++ is the only language supported by MICO. The three classes are depicted in Figure 3.4 (see the area between the two dashed lines). The class `Account` serves as a base class. It contains all the definitions belonging to the interface `Account`, like local declarations of user-defined data structures. This class also defines a pure virtual function for each operation contained in the interface. The following shows a bit of the code contained in class `Account`:

Class `Account`

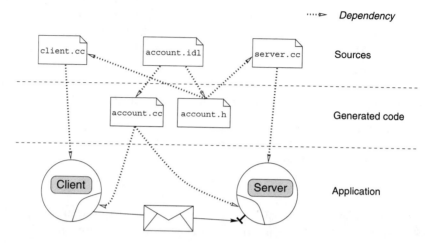

Figure 3.3
Creation process of a
MICO application

```
1:   // Code excerpt from account.h
2:   class Account : virtual public CORBA::Object {
3:       ...
4:   public:
5:       ...
6:       virtual void deposit( CORBA::ULong amount ) = 0;
7:       virtual void withdraw( CORBA::ULong amount ) = 0;
8:       virtual CORBA::Long balance() = 0;
9:   }
```

Class
Account_skel
    The class `Account_skel` is derived from `Account`. It adds a
dispatcher for the operations defined in class `Account`, but it does
not define the pure virtual functions of class `Account`. The classes
`Account` and `Account_skel` are therefore abstract base classes in
C++ terminology. To implement the account interface, you have
to make a subclass of class `Account_skel` providing implementations for the pure virtual methods `deposit()`, `withdraw()`, and
`balance()`.

Class
Account_stub
    The class `Account_stub` is derived from class `Account` as well.
In contrast to class `Account_skel`, it implements the pure virtual
functions. The implementation of these functions, which is automatically generated by the IDL compiler, is responsible for parameter marshalling. The code for `Account_stub` looks like this:

```
 1:   // Code excerpt from account.h and account.cc
 2:   class Account;
 3:   typedef Account *Account_ptr;
 4:
 5:   class Account_stub : virtual public Account {
 6:       ...
 7:   public:
 8:       ...
 9:       void deposit( CORBA::ULong amount )
10:       {
11:           // Marshalling code for deposit
12:       }
13:       void withdraw( CORBA::ULong amount )
14:       {
15:           // Marshalling code for withdraw
16:       }
17:       CORBA::Long balance()
18:       {
19:           // Marshalling code for balance
20:       }
21:   }
```

This makes Account_stub a concrete C++ class that can be instantiated. The programmer never uses the class Account_stub directly.
Access is provided only through class Account, as explained later.

It is worth seeing where the classes Account and Account_skel
are derived from. Account is inherited from Object, the base class
for all CORBA objects. This class is located in the MICO library. The more interesting inheritance path is for Account_skel.
Account_skel is inherited from StaticMethodDispatcher, again
a class located in the MICO library. This class is responsible for
dispatching a method invocation and maintains a list of method
dispatchers. In this example, the list contains only one dispatcher
for the Account object. In Section 5.5, when we discuss interface inheritance, this list will contain a dispatcher for each class
in the inheritance hierarchy. The class StaticMethodDispatcher
is inherited from StaticImplementation. This class mirrors the
behavior of the *Dynamic Skeleton Interface* (DSI) but is more effi-
ciently designed.

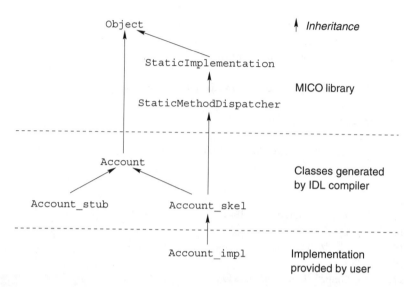

Figure 3.4
Inheritance relationship between stub and skeleton classes

MICO implementation of the bank account interface defined in account.idl

Until now, we have written the interface of an account object using CORBA IDL, saved it as `account.idl`, and run it through the IDL compiler, which left us with two files called `account.cc` and `account.h` that contain the class declarations for the account implementation base class (`Account_skel`) and the client stub (`Account_stub`). Figure 3.3 illustrates this. What is left to do is to subclass `Account_skel` (implementing the pure virtual methods) and write a program that uses the bank account. Here we go:

```
1: #include "account.h"
2:
3: class Account_impl : virtual public Account_skel
4: {
5: private:
6:   CORBA::Long _current_balance;
7:
8: public:
9:   Account_impl()
10:   {
11:     _current_balance = 0;
12:   };
```

```
13:    void deposit( CORBA::ULong amount )
14:    {
15:      _current_balance += amount;
16:    };
17:    void withdraw( CORBA::ULong amount )
18:    {
19:      _current_balance -= amount;
20:    };
21:    CORBA::Long balance()
22:    {
23:      return _current_balance;
24:    };
25: };
26:
27:
28: int main( int argc, char *argv[] )
29: {
30:    // ORB initialization
31:    CORBA::ORB_var orb =
32:            CORBA::ORB_init( argc, argv, "mico-local-orb" );
33:    CORBA::BOA_var boa =
34:            orb->BOA_init( argc, argv, "mico-local-boa" );
35:
36:    // server side
37:    Account_impl* server = new Account_impl;
38:    CORBA::String_var ref = orb->object_to_string( server );
39:    cout << "Server reference: " << ref << endl;
40:
41:    //---------------------------------------------------
42:
43:    // client side
44:    CORBA::Object_var obj = orb->string_to_object( ref );
45:    Account_var client = Account::_narrow( obj );
46:
47:    client->deposit( 700 );
48:    client->withdraw( 250 );
49:    cout << "Balance is " << client->balance() << endl;
50:
51:    // We don't need the server object anymore. This code
52:    // belongs to the server implementation
53:    CORBA::release( server );
54:    return 0;
55: }
```

Lines 3–25 contain the implementation of the account object, which is quite similar to the implementation in Section 3.3.1. Note that the class `Account_impl` is inherited from the class `Account_skel`, which contains the dispatcher for this interface, via a virtual public derivation. Although the keyword `virtual` is not required in this case, it is good practice to write it anyway. This will become important when interface inheritance is discussed in Section 5.5.

The `main()` function falls into two parts that are separated by the dashed line in line 41: above the separator is the server part that provides an account object, below the line is the client code that invokes methods on the account object provided by the server part. Theoretically, the two parts could be moved to two separate programs and run on two distinct machines, and almost nothing would have to be changed in the code. This will be shown in the next section.

Object Request Broker

In line 32, the MICO initialization function is used to obtain a pointer to the *Object Request Broker* (ORB) object—a central part of each CORBA implementation. Among other things, the ORB provides methods to convert object references into a string representation and vice versa. In line 37, an account object called `server` is instantiated. Note that it is not permitted to allocate CORBA objects on the runtime stack. This is because the CORBA standard prescribes that every object has to be deleted with a special function called `CORBA::release()`. Automatic allocation of an object would invoke its destructor when the program moved out of scope, which is not permissible. In our little sample program, the server object is deleted explicitly in line 53.

In line 38, the ORB is used to convert the object reference into a string that somehow has to be transmitted to the client (e.g., using a file, mail, a name service, or a trader). In our example, client and server run in the same address space (i.e., the same process), so we can turn the string back into an object reference again in line 44. Line 45 uses the `Account::_narrow()` method to downcast the object reference to an `Account_var`. The rest of `main()` just uses the account object instantiated in line 37.

`Account_var` is a smart pointer to `Account` instances. That is, an `Account_var` behaves like an `Account_ptr`, except that the storage of the referenced object is automatically freed via the release() function mentioned previously when the Account_var is destroyed. If you used Account_ptr instead, you would have to use CORBA::release() explicitly to free the object when you were done with it (*never* use delete instead of CORBA::release()).

Assuming the preceding code is saved to a file called account_impl.cc, you can compile the code like this:

```
mico-c++ -I. -c account_impl.cc -o account_impl.o
mico-c++ -I. -c account.cc -o account.o
mico-ld -I. -o account account_impl.o account.o -lmico<version>
```

mico-c++ and mico-ld are wrapper scripts for the C++ compiler and the linker; see Section 4.6 for details. The execution of these commands generates an executable called account. Running it produces the following output:

```
Server reference: IOR:010000001000000049444c3a4163636f756e\
743a312e30000200000000000000030000000010100001300000752d6d\
61792e7468696e6b6f6e652e636f6d00007b0900000c000000424f410a\
20b0530000055f0301000000240000000100000001000000100000014\
000000001000000010001000000000000901010000000000
Balance is 450
```

You can find the source code for this example in the demo/boa/account directory within the MICO source tree. The long hex dump is called *Interoperable Object Reference* (IOR), and it contains all the necessary address information a client requires in order to contact a server. Note that the IOR may look different on different systems. This is because it contains information that depends on the hostname, port number, and object identification for the server object, among other things. There is a tool called iordump (see directory mico/tools/iordump) that shows the content of the IOR. Feeding the preceding IOR into iordump yields the following output:

iordump *utility*

```
    Repo Id:  IDL:Account:1.0

IIOP Profile
    Version:  1.0
    Address:  inet:u-may.thinkone.com:2427
```

```
Location:   iioploc://u-may.thinkone.com:2427/\
               BOA%0a%20%b0S%00%00%05%5f%03
     Key:   42 4f 41 0a 20 b0 53 00 00 05 5f 03\
            BOA. .S..._.
```

```
Multiple Components Profile
 Components:  Native Codesets:
               normal: ISO 8859-1:1987; Latin Alphabet No. 1
                 wide: ISO/IEC 10646-1:1993; UTF-16,
                       UCS Transformation Format 16-bit form
     Key:  00
```

3.3.3   Separating client and server

CORBA would be pretty useless if you always had to run the object implementation (server) and the client that uses the server in the same process. Here is how to separate the client and server parts of the example in the previous section into two processes running either on the same machine or on different machines. You can also have some of the object implementations in one process and some in other processes. The ORB hides the actual locations of the object implementations from the user.

One problem you have to cope with when moving object implementation and client into separate address spaces is how the client gets to know the server. The solution to this problem is called a *naming service*.

Stringified object references

An object reference encodes the location of an object

The example presented in Section 3.3.2 used `object_to_string()` and `string_to_object()`, respectively, to make a stringified representation of an object reference and to turn this string back into an object.

Implementation of the account server

When separating client and server, you must find a way to transmit the stringified object reference from the server to the client. If client and server run on machines that share a single file system, you can make the server write the string into a file that is read by the client. Here's how to do it:

```
 1: // file account_server.cc
 2:
 3: #include <iostream.h>
 4: #include <fstream.h>
 5: #include "account.h"
 6:
 7: class Account_impl : virtual public Account_skel
 8: {
 9:   // unchanged, see section "MICO Application"
10:   // ...
11: };
12:
13:
14: int main( int argc, char *argv[] )
15: {
16:   // ORB initialization
17:   CORBA::ORB_var orb = CORBA::ORB_init( argc, argv, "mico-local-orb" );
18:   CORBA::BOA_var boa = orb->BOA_init( argc, argv, "mico-local-boa" );
19:
20:   Account_impl* server = new Account_impl;
21:   CORBA::String_var ref = orb->object_to_string( server );
22:   ofstream out ("/tmp/account.objid");
23:   out << ref << endl;
24:   out.close ();
25:
26:   boa->impl_is_ready( CORBA::ImplementationDef::_nil() );
27:   orb->run();
28:   CORBA::release( server );
29:   return 0;
30: }
```

Account_impl, the implementation of the account object in lines 7–11, is the same as in Section 3.3.2. The main() function performs ORB and BOA initialization in lines 16–18, which will evaluate and remove CORBA-specific command line options from argv (see Section 4.1.1 for details). In line 20, an account object is created. Lines 21–24 obtain a stringified object reference for this object and write it to a file called account.objid.

In line 26, the impl_is_ready() method of the BOA is called to activate the objects implemented by the server. The ORB method run(), which is invoked in line 27, will enter a loop to process incoming invocations. You can make run() return by calling the ORB method shutdown() (see Section 4.3.4 for details). Just before returning from main(), CORBA::release() is used in line 28 to destroy the account server object.

Implementation of the account client

```
1: // file account_client.cc
2:
3: #include <iostream.h>
4: #include <fstream.h>
5: #include "account.h"
6:
7: int main( int argc, char *argv[] )
8: {
9:    // ORB initialization
10:   CORBA::ORB_var orb = ...
11:   CORBA::BOA_var boa = ...
12:
13:   ifstream in ("/tmp/account.objid");
14:   char ref[1000];
15:   in >> ref;
16:   in.close ();
17:
18:   CORBA::Object_var obj = orb->string_to_object (ref);
19:   Account_var client = Account::_narrow( obj );
20:
21:   client->deposit( 700 );
22:   client->withdraw( 250 );
23:   cout << "Balance is " << client->balance() << endl;
24:
25:   return 0;
26: }
```

After ORB and BOA initialization, the client's main() function reads the stringified object reference in lines 13–16 and turns it back into an account object stub in lines 18–19. After it has made some method invocations in lines 21–23, client will be destroyed automatically because we have used an Account_var smart pointer. Note that this will only destroy the reference to the server, not the server itself.

Compile the client and server programs like this:

```
mico-c++ -I. -c account_server.cc -o account_server.o
mico-c++ -I. -c account_client.cc -o account_client.o
mico-c++ -I. -c account.cc -o account.o
mico-ld -o server account_server.o account.o -lmico<version>
mico-ld -o client account_client.o account.o -lmico<version>
```

First run **server** and then run **client** in a different shell. Make sure that the client and the server share the same **/tmp** directory. This is where the server stores its IOR in a file. The output from **client** will look like this:

```
Balance is 450
```

Note that running the client several times without restarting the server in between will increase the balance the client prints out by 450 each time! Note also that client and server do not necessarily have to run on the same machine. The stringified object reference, which is written to a file called **/tmp/account.objid**, contains the IP address and port number of the server's address. This way the client can locate the server over the network. The same example would also work in a heterogeneous environment. In that case, you would have to compile two versions of **account.o**, one for each hardware architecture. But the conversion of the parameters due to different data representations is taken care of by MICO.

MICO takes care of data conversions in a heterogeneous environment

Naming service

What we have actually done in the last section is to implement a very simple kind of naming service on top of the file system. A *naming service* is a mapping between names and addresses that allows you to look up the address for a given name. For example, a phone directory is a naming service: it maps people's names to phone numbers.

In the CORBA context, a naming service maps names to object references. The simple naming service we implemented in the previous section maps filenames to stringified object references. The OMG has defined a more elaborate naming service as a set of CORBA objects, an implementation of which is shipped with MICO. To use the naming service,

MICO contains a COSS-compliant naming service

❏   run the name service daemon **nsd**,

❏   tell server and client the address of **nsd** using the **-ORB-NamingAddr** option (see Section 4.1.1 for details),

❏   make the server register its offered objects with the naming service, and

❏   make the client query the name server for the server.

Chapter 7 gives a detailed discussion of the CORBA-compliant naming service that is part of the MICO distribution.

The MICO binder (CORBA extension)

There is still one problem left: how do you get an object reference for the naming service itself? This is especially problematic if the naming service and the client reside on machines that do not share a file system that could be used to pass around stringified object references, as in the previous section. The CORBA standard offers the ORB method **resolve_initial_references()** to obtain an object reference for the naming service. But that only moves the problem to the ORB instead of solving it. Because the CORBA standard does not offer a solution to this problem, MICO has to invent its own. Since it might be useful for other purposes as well, we decided to make the solution commonly available. Note that using this feature makes your programs incompatible with other CORBA implementations.

The ORB offers operations for obtaining initial references for certain objects

The MICO binder is a very simple naming service that maps (address, repository id) pairs to object references. A repository id is a string that identifies a CORBA IDL object and consists of the absolute name of the IDL object and a version number. Repository ids are generated by the IDL compiler. The repository id for the **Account** interface looks like this:

The MICO binder is a noncompliant, but easy-to-use, naming service

```
IDL:Account:1.0
```

An address identifies one process on one computer. MICO provides several kinds of addresses. The ones most commonly used are Internet addresses, Unix addresses, and local addresses. An *Internet address* is a string with the format inet:<host name>:<port number>

which refers to the process on machine <host name> that owns the TCP port <port number>. *Unix addresses* look like

unix:<socket file name>

and refer to the process on the current machine that owns the Unix-domain socket (Unix-domain sockets are named, bidirectional pipes) bound to <socket file name>. *Local addresses* look like

local:

and refer to the process they are used in (i.e., *this* process). Here is an adaptation of the account example that uses the MICO binder:

```
 1: // file account_server2.cc
 2:
 3: #include "account.h"
 4:
 5: class Account_impl : virtual public Account_skel
 6: {
 7:   // unchanged, see section "MICO Application"
 8:   // ...
 9: };
10:
11:
12: int main( int argc, char *argv[] )
13: {
14:   // ORB initialization
15:   CORBA::ORB_var orb =
16:       CORBA::ORB_init( argc, argv, "mico-local-orb" );
17:   CORBA::BOA_var boa =
18:       orb->BOA_init( argc, argv, "mico-local-boa" );
19:
20:   Account_impl* server = new Account_impl;
21:
22:   boa->impl_is_ready( CORBA::ImplementationDef::_nil() );
23:   orb->run();
24:   CORBA::release( server );
25:   return 0;
26: }
```

The server is essentially the same as in the subsection titled "Stringified object references" on page 36, except that it does not write a stringified object reference to a file. Here is the client:

```
1: // file account_client2.cc
2:
3: #include "account.h"
4:
5:
6: int main( int argc, char *argv[] )
7: {
8:    // ORB initialization
9:    CORBA::ORB_var orb = ...
10:   CORBA::BOA_var boa = ...
11:
12:   CORBA::Object_var obj
13:     = orb->bind ("IDL:Account:1.0", "inet:localhost:8888");
14:   if (CORBA::is_nil (obj)) {
15:      // no such object found ...
16:   }
17:   Account_var client = Account::_narrow( obj );
18:
19:   client->deposit( 700 );
20:   client->withdraw( 250 );
21:   cout << "Balance is " << client->balance() << endl;
22:
23:   return 0;
24: }
```

After completing ORB and BOA initialization, the client uses bind() to bind to an object with repository id IDL:Account:1.0 that is running in the process that owns port 8888 on the same machine (see line 13). Lines 14–16 check whether the bind failed. Everything else is the same as in the previous example. Compile

```
mico-c++ -I. -c account.cc -o account.o
mico-c++ -I. -c account_server2.cc -o account_server2.o
mico-c++ -I. -c account_client2.cc -o account_client2.o
mico-ld -o server2 account.o account_server2.o -lmico<version>
mico-ld -o client2 account.o account_client2.o -lmico<version>
```

Start the server like this, telling it to run on port number 8888:

```
./server2 -ORBIIOPAddr inet:localhost:8888
```

Run the client in a different shell without any arguments. It should behave the same way as the client from the previous example.

If a server offers several objects (say, A and B) of the same type (i.e., with the same repository id) and a client wants to bind to A, it needs a means to distinguish objects of the same type. This is accomplished by assigning objects an identifier during creation in the server and specifying this identifier as an extra argument to bind() in the client. The identifier is of type BOA::ReferenceData, which is a sequence of octets. You can use ORB::string_to_tag() and ORB::tag_to_string() to convert a string into such an identifier and vice versa. Here are the changes to the server code:

Distinguishing several instances of the same type using tags

```
 1: #include "account.h"
 2:
 3: class Account_impl : virtual public Account_skel {
 4: public:
 5:   Account_impl (const CORBA::BOA::ReferenceData &refdata)
 6:      : Account_skel (refdata)
 7:   {
 8:     _current_balance = 0;
 9:   }
10:   // remaining parts unchanged
11: };
12:
13: int main( int argc, char *argv[] )
14: {
15:   ...
16:   CORBA::BOA::ReferenceData_var id
17:     = CORBA::ORB::string_to_tag ("foo");
18:   Account_impl* server = new Account_impl (id);
19:   ...
20: }
```

Changes to the client code are as follows:

```
 1: #include "account.h"
 2:
 3: int main( int argc, char *argv[] )
```

```
 4: {
 5:   ...
 6:   CORBA::BOA::ReferenceData_var id
 7:     = CORBA::ORB::string_to_tag ("foo");
 8:   CORBA::Object_var obj = orb->
 9:     bind("IDL:Account:1.0", id, "inet:localhost:8888");
10:   ...
11: }
```

To avoid hardcoding the address of the server into the client, you can leave out the second argument to bind() and specify a list of addresses to try using the -ORBBindAddr command line option. For example,

```
./client -ORBBindAddr local: \
        -ORBBindAddr inet:localhost:8888
```

will make bind() try to bind to an account object in the same process, and if that fails, it will try to bind to an account object running in the server that owns port 8888 on the same machine. Note that addresses specified using -ORBBindAddr are taken into account only if you do not specify an explicit address.

The demo/boa/account2 directory contains an example that uses the MICO binder.

4   Implementation Overview

This chapter gives an overview of how MICO implements the COR-BA specification, the implementation components it consists of, and how those components are used.

A CORBA implementation consists of the following logical components:

Components of a CORBA implementation

❑   The Object Request Broker (ORB) provides for object location and method invocation.

❑   The Interface Repository (IR) stores runtime type information.

❑   One or more *object adapters* form the interface between object implementations and the ORB. MICO provides the Basic Object Adapter (BOA) and Portable Object Adapter (POA). The *implementation repository* stores information about how to activate object implementations.

❑   The *IDL compiler* generates client stubs, server skeletons, and marshalling code from a CORBA IDL according to the supported language mappings.

Each of these logical components has to be mapped to one or more implementation components, which are described in the next sections.

4.1   ORB

The ORB is implemented as a library (`libmico<version>.a`) that is linked into each MICO application.

MICO library
`libmico<version>.a`

4.1.1   ORB initialization

Every MICO application has to call the ORB initialization function `ORB_init()` before using MICO functionality.

```
1:   int main (int argc, char *argv[])
2:   {
3:      CORBA::ORB_var orb =
4:              CORBA::ORB_init (argc, argv, "mico-local-orb");
5:      ...
6:   }
```

That way the ORB has access to the application's command line arguments. After evaluating them, the ORB removes the command line options it understands so the application does not have to bother with them. You can also put ORB command line arguments into a file called `.micorc` in your home directory. Arguments given on the command line override settings from `.micorc`. Here is a description of all ORB-specific command line arguments:

Command line arguments understood by MICO applications

-ORBNoIIOPServer

Do not activate the IIOP server. The IIOP server enables other processes to invoke methods on objects in this process using the Internet Inter-ORB Protocol (IIOP). If for some reason you do not want other processes to be able to invoke objects in this process, use this option. The default is to activate the IIOP server.

-ORBNoIIOPProxy

Do not activate the IIOP proxy. The IIOP proxy enables this process to invoke methods on objects in other processes using IIOP. If you do not want or need this, use this option. The default is to activate the IIOP proxy.

-ORBIIOPAddr <address>

Set the address the IIOP server should run on (see Section 3.3.3 for details on addresses). If you do not specify this option, the IIOP server will choose an unused address. This option can be used more than once to make the server listen on several addresses (e.g., a `unix:` and an `inet:` address).

-ORBIIOPBlocking
> Make IIOP use sockets in blocking mode. This gains some extra performance, but nested method invocations do not work in this mode.

-ORBId <ORB identifier>
> Specify the ORB identifier; `mico-local-orb` is currently the only supported ORB identifier. This option is intended for programs that need access to different CORBA implementations in the same process. In this case, the option `-ORBId` is used to select one of the CORBA implementations.

-ORBImplRepoIOR <impl repository IOR>
> Specify a stringified object reference for the implementation repository the ORB should use.

-ORBImplRepoAddr <impl repository address>
> Specify the address of a process that runs an implementation repository. The ORB will then try to bind to an implementation repository object using the given address (see Section 3.3.3 for details on addresses and the binder). If the bind fails or if you specified neither `-ORBImplRepoAddr` nor `-ORBImpRepoIOR`, the ORB will run a local implementation repository.

-ORBIfaceRepoIOR <interface repository IOR>
> The same as `-ORBImplRepoIOR` but for the interface repository.

-ORBIfaceRepoAddr <interface repository address>
> The same as `-ORBImplRepoAddr` but for the interface repository.

-ORBNamingIOR <naming service IOR>
> The same as `-ORBImplRepoIOR` but for the naming service.

-ORBNamingAddr <naming address>
> The same as `-ORBImplRepoAddr` but for the naming service.

-ORBInitRef <Identifier>=<IOR>
> Set the value for the initial reference by the name of `identifier`

to the given object reference. This mechanism can be used both for custom and for standard initial references.

-ORBDefaultInitRef <IOR-base>

Define a location for initial references. `IOR-base` is an `iioploc`- or `iiopname`-style object reference. When a previously unknown initial reference is searched for using `resolve_initial_references()`, the searched-for identifier is concatenated to the `IOR-base` string to produce the service's location.

-ORBNoResolve

Do not resolve given IP addresses into hostnames. Use dotted decimal notation instead.

-ORBDebugLevel <level>

Specify the debug level. `<level>` is a nonnegative integer with greater values giving more debug output on `cerr`.

-ORBBindAddr <address>

Specify an address that `bind(const char *repoid)` should try to bind to. This option can be used more than once to specify multiple addresses.

-ORBConfFile <rcfile>

Specify the file from which to read additional command line options (defaults to `~/.micorc`).

-ORBNoCodeSets

Do not add code set information to object references. Since code set conversion is a CORBA 2.1 feature, this option may be needed to talk to ORBs that are not CORBA 2.1 compliant. Furthermore, it may gain some extra speed.

-ORBNativeCS <pattern>

Specify the code set the application uses for characters and strings. `<pattern>` is a shell-like pattern that must match the `description` field of a code set in the OSF code set registry. For example, the pattern `*8859-1*` will make the ORB use the code set ISO-8859-1 (Latin 1) as the native char code set, which is the default if you do not specify this option. The

ORB uses this information to automatically convert characters and strings when talking to an application that uses a
different code set.

-ORBNativeWCS <pattern>
Similar to -ORBNativeCS, but it specifies the code set the application uses for wide characters and wide strings. Defaults
to UTF-16, a 16-bit encoding of Unicode.

4.1.2   Obtaining initial references

The ORB offers a function for obtaining object references for the
interface repository, the implementation repository, and other well-
known services. Here is an example that shows how to obtain
a reference for the interface repository using resolve_initial_
references():

*Object references
for standard
components can be
requested from the
ORB*

```
 1:  int main (int argc, char *argv[])
 2:  {
 3:    CORBA::ORB_var orb =
 4:      CORBA::ORB_init (argc, argv, "mico-local-orb");
 5:    ...
 6:    CORBA::Object_var obj =
 7:      orb->resolve_initial_references ("InterfaceRepository");
 8:    CORBA::Repository_var repo =
 9:      CORBA::Repository::_narrow (obj);
10:    ...
11:  }
```

If you specify the interface repository by using the ORB command line option -ORBIfaceRepoAddr or -ORBIfaceRepoIOR, the
reference returned from resolve_initial_references() will be
the one you specified. Otherwise, the ORB will run a local interface repository and you will get a reference to this one. Obtaining
a reference to the implementation repository ("Implementation
Repository") and the naming service ("NameService") works the
same way as for the interface repository. There is another method
that returns a list of names called list_initial_services(),
which can be used as arguments for resolve_initial_
references(). Here's how to use it:

```
 1:  int main (int argc, char *argv[])
 2:  {
 3:    CORBA::ORB_var orb =
 4:      CORBA::ORB_init (argc, argv, "mico-local-orb");
 5:    ...
 6:    CORBA::ORB::ObjectIdList_var ids =
 7:      orb->list_initial_services();
 8:    for( int i = 0; i < ids->length(); i++ )
 9:      cout << ids[ i ] << endl;
10:    ...
11:  }
```

Initial references can also be specified using the -ORBInitRef and -ORBDefaultInitRef command line options.

4.2   Interface Repository (IR)

The IR stores runtime type information

The interface repository is implemented by a separate program (ird). The idea is to run one instance of the program and make all MICO applications use the same interface repository. As we mentioned in Section 4.1.2, the command line option -ORBIfaceRepo Addr can be used to tell a MICO application which interface repository to use. But where do you get the address of the ird program? The solution is to tell ird an address it should bind to by using the -ORBIIOPAddr. Here is an example of how to run ird:

```
ird -ORBIIOPAddr inet:<ird-host-name>:8888
```

where <ird-host-name> should be replaced by the name of the host executing ird. Afterward you can run MICO applications this way:

```
some_mico_application -ORBIfaceRepoAddr \
                      inet:<ird-host-name>:8888
```

To avoid typing in such long command lines, you can put the option into the file .micorc in your home directory:

```
echo -ORBIfaceRepoAddr inet:<ird-host-name>:8888 \
                      > ~/.micorc
```

Now you can just type

```
some_mico_application
```

and `some_mico_application` will still use the `ird`'s interface repository.

The following command line arguments control `ird`:

`--help`

> Show a list of all supported command line arguments and exit.

`--db <database file>`

> Specify the filename where `ird` should save the contents of the interface repository when exiting. `ird` is terminated by pressing `ctrl-c` or by sending it the `SIGTERM` signal. When `ird` is restarted afterward, it will read the file given by the `--db` option to restore the contents of the interface repository. Notice that the contents of this database file is just plain ASCII representing a CORBA IDL specification.

4.3   BOA

The Basic Object Adapter (BOA) was the only object adapter specified by CORBA up to version 2.1 of the specification. One of its main features is the ability to *activate* object implementations when their service is requested by a client. This basically means running a program that implements an object. Using the implementation repository, the BOA decides how an object implementation has to be activated (i.e., which program has to be run with which options and which activation policy has to be used for the implementation).

To fulfill these requirements of the CORBA specification, the BOA is implemented partially by a library (`libmico<version>.a`) and partially by a separate program (`micod`) called the *BOA daemon*.

*The Basic Object
Adapter (BOA) is
responsible for the
activation of
objects*

4.3.1 BOA initialization

Like the ORB initialization described in Section 4.1.1, the BOA
has to be initialized like this:

```
int main( int argc, char *argv[] )
{
  CORBA::ORB_var orb =
    CORBA::ORB_init( argc, argv, "mico-local-orb" );
  CORBA::BOA_var boa =
    orb->BOA_init( argc, argv, "mico-local-boa" );
  ...
}
```

Thus, it has access to the application's command line arguments.
After evaluating them, the BOA will remove the command line
options it knows about from `argv`. As for the ORB, you can put
BOA-specific command line options into a file called `.micorc` in
your home directory. Arguments given on the command line override settings from `.micorc`. Here is a list of command line options
the BOA understands:

Command line
options controlling
BOA behavior

-OAId <BOA identifier>
> This option specifies the BOA identifier; `mico-local-boa` is
> the only currently supported BOA identifier.

-OAImplName <name of the object implementation>
> This option tells a server its implementation name. It must be
> used when launching a persistent server that should register
> with the BOA daemon.

-OARestoreIOR <IOR to restore>
> This option is part of the interface between the BOA daemon
> and an object implementation. Do not use this option!

-OARemoteIOR <remote BOA IOR>
> This option is part of the interface between the BOA daemon
> and an object implementation. Do not use this option!

-OARemoteAddr <remote BOA address>
> This option tells an object implementation the address of the

BOA daemon. You should use this option only when starting persistent servers that should register with the BOA daemon (see Section 4.3.4 for details).

4.3.2 BOA daemon

The BOA daemon (`micod`) is the part of the basic object adapter that activates object implementations when their service is requested. `micod` also contains the implementation repository. To make all MICO applications use a single implementation repository, take similar actions as for the interface repository described in Section 4.2. That is, tell `micod` an address to bind to using the `-ORBIIOPAddr` option and tell all MICO applications this address by using the option `-ORBImplRepoAddr`. For example:

```
micod -ORBIIOPAddr inet:<micod-host-name>:9999
```

Now you can run all MICO applications like this:

```
some_mico_application -ORBImplRepoAddr \
                    inet:<micod-host-name>:9999
```

or put the option into `.micorc` and run `some_mico_application` without arguments.

> `micod` understands the following command line arguments:

Command line options understood by `micod`

`--help`

> Show a list of all supported command line arguments and exit.

`--forward`

> Instruct `micod` to make use of GIOP location forwarding, which results in much better performance (almost no overhead compared to not using `micod` at all). Unfortunately, this requires some client-side GIOP features that some ORBs do not support properly although prescribed in the CORBA specification. Therefore, you may encounter problems when using clients implemented using such broken ORBs. That is why this feature is off by default.

--db <database file>

> Specify the filename where micod should save the contents of the implementation repository when exiting. micod is terminated by pressing ctrl-c or by sending it the SIGTERM signal. When micod is restarted afterward, it will read the file given by the --db option to restore the contents of the implementation repository.

4.3.3   Implementation Repository (IMR)

The implementation repository is the place where information about an object implementation (also known as a server) is stored. The CORBA specification only gives you an idea of what the implementation repository is for and does not specify the interface to it. So the design of the implementation repository is specific to MICO. Here's the IDL for MICO's implementation repository:

MICO-specific interface to the Implementation Repository

```
 1:  module CORBA {
 2:      /*
 3:       * Implementation Repository Entry
 4:       */
 5:      interface ImplementationDef {
 6:
 7:          enum ActivationMode {
 8:              ActivateShared,
 9:              ActivateUnshared,
10:              ActivatePerMethod,
11:              ActivatePersistent,
12:              ActivateLibrary,
13:              ActivatePOA
14:          };
15:
16:          typedef sequence<octet> ObjectTag;
17:
18:          struct ObjectInfo {
19:              string repoid;
20:              ObjectTag tag;
21:          };
22:
23:          typedef sequence<ObjectInfo> ObjectInfoList;
24:
```

```
25:          attribute ActivationMode mode;
26:          attribute ObjectInfoList objs;
27:          readonly attribute string name;
28:          attribute string command;
29:          readonly attribute string tostring;
30:      };
31:
32:      /*
33:       * Implementation Repository
34:       */
35:      interface ImplRepository {
36:        typedef sequence<ImplementationDef> ImplDefSeq;
37:
38:        ImplementationDef create (...);
39:        void destroy (in ImplementationDef impl_def);
40:        ImplDefSeq find_by_name (in string name);
41:        ImplDefSeq find_by_repoid (in string repoid);
42:        ImplDefSeq find_all ();
43:      };
44:  };
```

The interface `ImplRepository` defined in lines 35–43 is the implementation repository itself. It contains methods for creating, destroying, and finding entries. An implementation repository entry is defined by the interface `ImplementationDef` in lines 5–30. There is exactly one entry for each server, which contains the

Information maintained for each server by IMR

❏   name,

❏   activation mode,

❏   shell command or loadable module path, and

❏   list of repository ids (and tags)

for the server. The name uniquely identifies the server. The activation mode tells the BOA whether the server should be activated once (*shared server*), once for each object instance (*unshared server*), once for each method invocation (*per-method server*), or not at all (*persistent server*) (see Section 4.3.4 for details on activation modes). The shell command is executed by the BOA whenever the server has to be (re)started. Activation mode *library* is used for

Activation modes

loading servers into the same process as the client during runtime. Instead of a shell command, specify the path of the loadable server module for library activation mode. Finally, there is a repository id (and optionally a tag to distinguish several implementations of the same interface) for each IDL interface implemented by the server (see Section 3.3.3 for details on repository ids).

If you have written a server that should be activated by the BOA daemon when its service is requested, you have to create an entry for that server. This can be accomplished by using the program `imr`. `imr` can be used to list all entries in the implementation repository, to show detailed information for one entry, to create a new entry, or to delete an entry. The implementation repository is selected by the options `-ORBImplRepoAddr` or `-ORBImplRepoIOR`, which you usually put into your `.micorc` file.

Listing all entries

Just issue the command `imr list` to get a listing of the names of all entries in the implementation repository.

Details for one entry

`imr info <name>` shows detailed information for the entry named `<name>`.

Creating new entries

The command

```
imr create <name> <mode> <command> \
    <repoid1[#tag1]> <repoid2[#tag1]> ...
```

creates a new entry with name `<name>`. `<mode>` is one of the following:

❑ persistent

❑ shared

❑ unshared

❑ permethod

❏ `library`

❏ `poa`

`<command>` is the shell command that should be used to start the server. Note that all paths have to be absolute since `micod`'s current directory is probably different from your current directory. Furthermore, make sure that the server is located on the same machine as `micod`, otherwise you should use `rsh`; see below for examples. `<repoid1[#tag1]>`, `<repoid2[#tag2]>`, and so on are the repository ids (and, optionally, tags for distinguishing several implementations of the same interface) for the IDL interfaces implemented by the server.

Deleting entries

`imr delete <name>` deletes the entry named `<name>`.

Forcing activation of an implementation

Registering an implementation in the implementation repository does not automatically activate the implementation. Usually, the BOA daemon only activates a nonpersistent implementation when its service is requested by a client. But sometimes you have to force activation of an implementation, for instance, to make the implementation register itself with a naming service. `imr activate <name> [<micod-address>]` activates the implementation named `<name>`. To do so, however, `imr` needs to know the address of the BOA daemon. Usually, this is the same address as for the implementation repository and you do not need to specify `<micod-address>`. Only if the BOA daemon is bound to an address different from the implementation repository address and different from the addresses specified using the `-ORBBindAddr` option must you specify `<micod-address>` as a command line option to `imr`.

Examples

Assume we want to register the account server `account_server2` from Section 3.3.3 as a shared server. Assume as well that neither micod nor ird has been started yet, so we have to get them running first. If the hostname were zirkon, you would do the following:

```
# create .micorc (only do that once)
echo -ORBIfaceRepoAddr inet:zirkon:9000 > ~/.micorc
echo -ORBImplRepoAddr inet:zirkon:9001 >> ~/.micorc

# run ird
ird -ORBIIOPAddr inet:zirkon:9000

# run micod in a different shell
micod -ORBIIOPAddr inet:zirkon:9001
```

Now we are prepared to create the implementation repository entry for account_server2. Recall that this server implemented the interface Account whose repository id is IDL:Account:1.0. If the server account_server2 has been copied to /usr/bin, you can create the implementation repository entry using the following command:

```
imr create Account shared /usr/bin/account_server2 \
        IDL:Account:1.0
```

If account_server2 is located on host diamant (i.e., *not* on zirkon), use the rsh command. This requires of course that you have entries in your .rhosts file that allow micod to execute programs on diamant. Here is the command to create the implementation repository entry:

```
imr create Account shared \
        "rsh diamant /usr/bin/account_server2" \
        IDL:Account:1.0
```

Now you should change account_client2.cc to bind to the address of micod. Note that you no longer need to know the address of the account server account_server2 but only need to know the address of micod. Here is the part of account_client2.cc that has to be changed:

```
1:  // account_client2.cc
2:  ...
3:    CORBA::Object_var obj =
4:      orb->bind ("IDL:Account:1.0", "inet:zirkon:9001");
5:  ...
```

Running the recompiled client automatically activates the server `account_server2`.

Creating an entry for a loadable module (library activation mode) looks like this if `/usr/local/lib/module.so` is the path to the module:

```
imr create Account library /usr/local/lib/module.so \
        IDL:Account:1.0
```

Make sure that a loadable module and any client that wants to make use of the module reside on the same machine.

4.3.4 Activation modes

As mentioned in the previous section, the BOA supports several activation modes. Using them is not simply a matter of creating an implementation repository entry, as an object implementation has to use special BOA functionality according to the selected activation mode. This section gives details on the various activation modes available.

Activation mode shared

Shared servers can serve any number of object instances, which is probably the most widely used approach. The account server from Section 3.3.3 is an example of a shared server. Let's look at the code again:

Shared servers host multiple objects

```
1: // file account_server2.cc
2:
3: #include "account.h"
4:
5: class Account_impl : virtual public Account_skel
6: {
7:   // unchanged, see section "MICO Application"
```

```
 8:   // ...
 9: };
10:
11:
12: int main( int argc, char *argv[] )
13: {
14:    // ORB initialization
15:    CORBA::ORB_var orb = CORBA::ORB_init( ... );
16:    CORBA::BOA_var boa = orb->BOA_init( ... );
17:
18:    Account_impl* server = new Account_impl;
19:
20:    boa->impl_is_ready( CORBA::ImplementationDef::_nil() );
21:    orb->run();
22:    CORBA::release( server );
23:    return 0;
24: }
```

After creating the implementation repository entry for the account server using the `imr` utility, the account server stays inactive until the account client wants to bind to an object with repository id `IDL:Account:1.0`. The BOA daemon recognizes that there are no active account objects and consults the implementation repository for servers that implement objects with repository id `IDL:Account:1.0`. It will find the account server and run it. The account server in turn creates an account object in line 18, which will be announced to the BOA daemon. The server uses `impl_is_ready()` to tell the BOA daemon that it has completed initialization and is prepared to receive method invocations. The BOA daemon in turn finds the newly created account object and answers the bind request from the client with it. Finally, `run()` is called on the ORB to start processing incoming requests.

`run()` will wait for requests and serve them as they arrive until the `deactivate_impl()` method is called, which deactivates the server. Calling the ORB method `shutdown()` will make `run()` return, and the account server will exit. If method invocations arrive after the server has exited, the BOA daemon will restart the server (see Section 4.3.5 for details on restarting servers).

There are many reasons for calling `deactivate_impl()`. For example, we could augment the account objects interface by a management interface that offers a method `exit()` that will shut down the account server:

```
1:   // account.idl
2:   interface Account {
3:     ...
4:     void exit ();
5:   };
```

The implementation of the `exit()` method would look like this:

```
1:   class Account_impl : virtual public Account_skel {
2:     ...
3:   public:
4:     ...
5:     virtual void exit ()
6:     {
7:       CORBA::BOA_var boa = _boa();
8:       CORBA::ORB_var orb = _orb();
9:       boa->deactivate_impl (CORBA::ImplementationDef::_nil());
10:      orb->shutdown (TRUE);
11:    }
12:  };
```

Note that we passed a NIL `ImplementationDef` to `deactivate _impl()` as well as to `impl_is_ready()`. Usually, the implementation repository has to be searched to find the entry for the server and pass it. When passing NIL, the entry will be searched by the BOA. `shutdown()` has a boolean `wait` parameter that controls whether the ORB should immediately stop processing events (`wait=FALSE`) or wait until all pending requests have completed (`wait=TRUE`).

Activation mode persistent

Persistent servers are just like shared servers, except that the BOA daemon does not activate them. Instead, they are started by means outside of the BOA, for example, by a system administrator or a shell script. The code of a persistent server looks exactly like that of a shared server. But note that once `deactivate_impl()` and `shutdown()` are called, the server will *not* be restarted by the BOA daemon.

Persistent servers are not started by the BOA daemon

Thus, persistent servers do not need a running BOA daemon. Clients can connect directly to the object implementation, yielding better performance (see Section 3.3.3 for an example). However, there is still a reason to have persistent servers register with the BOA daemon: you can do a `bind()` using the address of the BOA daemon, so you do not need to know the address of the persistent server. To make a persistent server register with the BOA daemon, do this:

```
some_server -OARemoteAddr <micod-address> \
            -ORBImplRepoAddr <micod-address> \
            -OAImplName <impl-name>
```

where `<micod-address>` is the address `micod` is bound to. This is usually the same address you used as an argument to `-ORBIIOPAddr` when starting `micod` (see Section 3.3.3 for details on addresses and Sections 4.1.1 and 4.3.1 for details on command line arguments). The name `<impl-name>` of the entry in the implementation repository corresponds to the server.

Activation mode unshared

Unshared servers host only one object

Unshared servers are similar to shared servers. The difference is that each instance of an unshared server can serve only one object instance: that is, for N objects you need N running instances of an unshared server.

Further, you cannot use the functions `impl_is_ready()` and `deactivate_impl()`. Instead, you have to use `obj_is_ready()` and `deactivate_obj()`. Here is the `main()` function of an unshared account server:

```
1: // file account_server2.cc
2:
3: #include "account.h"
4:
5: class Account_impl : virtual public Account_skel
6: {
7:   // unchanged, see section "MICO Application"
8:   // ...
9: };
10:
```

```
11:
12: int main( int argc, char *argv[] )
13: {
14:   // ORB initialization
15:   CORBA::ORB_var orb = CORBA::ORB_init( ... );
16:   CORBA::BOA_var boa = orb->BOA_init( ... );
17:
18:   Account_impl* server = new Account_impl;
19:
20:   boa->obj_is_ready(server,CORBA::ImplementationDef::_nil());
21:   orb->run();
22:   CORBA::release( server );
23:   return 0;
24: }
```

The `exit()` method would look like this in an unshared server:

```
1:  class Account_impl : virtual public Account_skel {
2:     ...
3:  public:
4:     ...
5:     virtual void exit ()
6:     {
7:       CORBA::BOA_var boa = _boa();
8:       CORBA::ORB_var orb = _orb();
9:       boa->deactivate_obj (this);
10:      orb->shutdown (TRUE);
11:    }
12:  };
```

Although an unshared server instance can *serve* only one object instance, it can *create* more than one object instance. Imagine, for example, a bank object

```
1:  // bank.idl
2:  interface Bank {
3:    Account create ();
4:    void destroy (in Account account);
5:  };
```

that can create new account objects and destroy account objects that are no longer needed. Such a design pattern is called a *factory*.　　*Factory objects*

The implementation of the `create()` method in an unshared server would look like this:

```
1:   // bank_server.cc
2:   class Bank_impl : virtual public Bank_skel {
3:      ...
4:   public:
5:      ...
6:     virtual Account_ptr create ()
7:     {
8:        Account_ptr account = new Account_impl;
9:
10:       CORBA::BOA_var boa = _boa();
11:       boa->deactivate_obj (account);
12:
13:       return Account::_duplicate (account);
14:     }
15:   };
```

Note that line 11 calls `deactivate_obj()` on the newly created object. This will tell the BOA daemon that you are not going to serve this object; instead, a new server instance has to be activated to serve the newly created account object. For this to work, implement saving and restoring for your objects as described in Section 4.3.5. If you delete lines 10 and 11, you will get the code for `create()` in a shared or persistent server.

Accessing newly created objects from within the server

If you need access to the newly created account object from within the server where it was first created, you must take special actions. This is because the created account object is initially an account object implementation (`Account_impl`), but in order to access the moved account object in the other server, you need an account stub (`Account_stub`). Here's how to create this stub:

```
1:   // bank_server.cc
2:   class Bank_impl : virtual public Bank_skel {
3:      ...
4:   public:
5:      ...
6:     virtual Account_ptr create ()
7:     {
8:        CORBA::BOA_var boa = _boa();
```

```
 9:        CORBA::ORB_var orb = _orb();
10:
11:        Account_ptr account = new Account_impl;
12:        boa->deactivate_obj (account);
13:
14:        // turn 'account' into a stub
15:        CORBA::String_var ref = orb->object_to_string(account);
16:        CORBA::release (account);
17:        CORBA::Object_var obj = orb->string_to_object (ref);
18:        account = Account::_narrow (obj);
19:
20:        // now you can invoke methods on (the remote) 'account'
21:        account->deposit (100);
22:
23:        return Account::_duplicate (account);
24:    }
25: };
```

The demo/boa/account3 directory contains a complete example for an unshared server that creates more than one object.

Activation mode per method

Per-method servers are similar to unshared servers, except that a
new server instance is launched for each method invocation. The
code for a per-method server looks the same as for an unshared
server. But note that run() will return after the first method
invocation, whereas in an unshared server run() will not return
until you call shutdown().

*Per-method servers
are activated for
each operation*

Activation mode library

All activation modes discussed so far assume client and server to be
different programs that run in separate processes. This approach
has the advantage that client and server can be bound to each other
dynamically during runtime. The drawback is the overhead for doing method invocations across process boundaries using some kind
of interprocess communication (IPC). The activation mode *library*
eliminates this drawback while still allowing runtime binding. This
is achieved by loading an object implementation (called a *module*

*Activation mode
library is MICO
specific*

from now on) into the running client. Invoking methods on an object loaded this way is as fast as a C++ method invocation.

A client intended to use this feature does not differ from other clients; only the loadable module requires special code, and you have to create a special entry in the implementation repository. For example, let's change the bank account example from Section 3.3.3 to make use of dynamic loading. The only change in the client is the address specified in the call to bind(): we have to use "local:" instead of "inet:localhost:8888", because we want to bind to the dynamically loaded object running in the same process:

```
 1: // file account_client2.cc
 2:
 3: #include "account.h"
 4:
 5:
 6: int main( int argc, char *argv[] )
 7: {
 8:   // ORB initialization
 9:   CORBA::ORB_var orb = ...
10:   CORBA::BOA_var boa = ...
11:
12:   CORBA::Object_var obj
13:     = orb->bind ("IDL:Account:1.0", "local:");
14:   if (CORBA::is_nil (obj)) {
15:     // no such object found ...
16:   }
17:   Account_var client = Account::_narrow( obj );
18:
19:   client->deposit( 700 );
20:   client->withdraw( 250 );
21:   cout << "Balance is " << client->balance() << endl;
22:
23:   return 0;
24: }
```

Here's the code for the loadable module:

```
0: // file module.cc
1:
2: #include "account.h"
3: #include <mico/template_impl.h>
```

```
 4:
 5: class Account_impl : virtual public Account_skel
 6: {
 7:   // unchanged, see section "MICO Application"
 8:   // ...
 9: };
10:
11: static Account_ptr server = Account::_nil();
12:
13: extern "C" CORBA::Boolean
14: mico_module_init (const char *version)
15: {
16:   if (strcmp (version, MICO_VERSION))
17:     return FALSE;
18:   server = new Account_impl;
19:   return TRUE;
20: }
21:
22: extern "C" void
23: mico_module_exit ()
24: {
25:   CORBA::release (server);
26: }
```

Lines 13–20 define a function `mico_module_init()` that is called
when the module is loaded into the running client. Note that this
function must be declared as `extern "C"` to avoid C++ name man-
gling. The `version` argument to `mico_module_init()` is a string   *Modules require*
specifying the MICO version of the client the module is loaded in-   *support for shared*
to. Lines 16 and 17 check if this version is the same as the MICO   *libraries*
version the module was compiled with, and make module initialization fail by returning `FALSE` if they differ. Otherwise, a new
account object is created and `TRUE` is returned, indicating successful module initialization. Note that `mico_module_init()` must not
perform ORB and BOA initialization since the client the module
is loaded into did this already. The function `mico_module_exit()`
is called just before the module is unloaded from the client and
should release all allocated resources: in our example, the account
object created in `mico_module_init()`. `mico_module_exit()` is
only called if `mico_module_init()` returns `TRUE`. Modules have to

Mode	Description
Shared	Server is shared among several clients
Persistent	Server is started manually
Unshared	Each client is using a different server
Method	Each method invocation starts a server
Library	Server is located in shared library and loaded on demand
POA	Shared server that uses the POA

Table 4.1
*Activation modes
supported by MICO*

be compiled as a shared library; see Section 4.6 for details and an example.

Although communication does not go through the BOA daemon when using loadable modules, you need a running `micod` because you have to create an implementation repository entry for the module. See Section 4.3.3 for details. The directory `demo/shlib` contains a complete example.

Table 4.1 summarizes the different features of the various activation modes.

4.3.5   Making objects persistent

The CORBA specification gives only a vague idea of object persistence and omits any implementation details. That is why everything explained in this section is specific to MICO and will not work with other CORBA implementations. In the last section, we saw two cases where an object had to be "moved" between two different instances of a server:

*Support for object
persistence is
specific to MICO*

❑   If an unshared or per-method server creates a second object, it has to be moved to a new server instance.

❑   If a server terminates and is restarted later, all the objects of the terminated server have to be moved to the restarted server.

In both cases, the state of the moved object has to be saved before and restored after moving. Because the BOA has no information about the internal state of an object, you have to provide code for saving and restoring. However, the BOA offers some support methods.

Saving is done in the `_save_object()` method of the object implementation. If you do not provide this method for an object, `_save_object()` from the base class will be used, which will cause the object to be treated as transient (i.e., it will not be restored later). Let us again consider the account example. The internal state of an account object consists of the current balance. Here's how to save the state:

Saving an object's state

```
1:  // account_server3.cc
2:
3:  #include "account.h"
4:  #include <iostream.h>
5:  #include <fstream.h>
6:
7:  class Account_impl : virtual public Account_skel {
8:    CORBA::Long _current_balance;
9:  public:
10:    ...
11:    virtual CORBA::Boolean _save_object ()
12:    {
13:      ofstream out (_ident());
14:      out << _current_balance;
15:      return TRUE;
16:    }
17:  };
```

Pretty simple! We just open a file and write the balance into it. The only noteworthy thing is the filename, which is obtained by using the `_ident()` method. The returned string is guaranteed to be unique among all objects managed by a single BOA daemon. If you use multiple BOA daemons or use persistent servers that do not register with the BOA, you should make sure no name clashes occur. One way to do this is to create a new directory where all the files are created; in our example, `/tmp/account/` would be appropriate. Another way to distinguish different instances (objects) of an interface (class) is to use `BOA::ReferenceData`. See `demo/boa/account2` for an example.

Restoring the state takes a bit more code. You need to subclass the abstract base class `CORBA::BOAObjectRestorer` providing an implementation for the `restore()` method:

Restoring an object's state

```
1:   // account_server3.cc
2:
3:   class AccountLoader : public CORBA::BOAObjectRestorer {
4:   public:
5:     CORBA::Boolean restore (CORBA::Object_ptr obj)
6:     {
7:        if (!strcmp (obj->_repoid(), "IDL:Account:1.0")) {
8:          new Account_impl (obj);
9:          return TRUE;
10:       }
11:       // don't know about such objects
12:       return FALSE;
14:     }
15:   };
```

`restore()` receives an object reference for the object that has to be restored. We use the `_repoid()` method to find out the repository id of the object to be restored (see Section 3.3.3 for details on repository ids). If it is equal to the repository id of account objects (`"IDL:Account:1.0"`), we can go on with restoring; otherwise, we just return FALSE, indicating that we cannot restore the object.

Restoring the object is now just a matter of calling a special `Account_impl` constructor, which we still have to define:

```
1:   // account_server3.cc
2:
3:   class Account_impl : virtual public Account_skel {
4:     CORBA::Long _current_balance;
5:   public:
6:     ...
7:     Account_impl (CORBA::Object_ptr obj)
8:       : Account_skel (obj)
9:     {
10:       ifstream in (obj->_ident());
11:       in >> _current_balance;
12:     }
13:   };
```

The constructor is basically the counterpart to _save_object().
It uses _ident() to obtain the identification string of the object
to be restored, opens the associated file, and reads in the current
balance. Note the invocation of the base class constructor in line
8, which is very important. If you forget this line, the code will
still compile but will give you strange results because the default
Account_skel constructor will be used, which is an error. Note
that we have omitted error handling for ease of exposition. Usually,
you would check whether the file exists and whether its contents
are valid. You should make AccountLoader::restore() return
FALSE if an error is detected.

Finally, you have to create an instance of the AccountLoader
class. Note that you have to create at least one such instance *before*
you do ORB and BOA initialization because restoring can already
occur during BOA initialization. Of course, you can create several different BOAObjectRestorer subclasses, each of which handles
special kinds of objects. When an object has to be restored, the
restore() methods of the existing restorer objects are called until eventually one returns TRUE. Note that you should not create
new objects if any objects are being restored; otherwise, you would
get an infinitely growing number of objects over time. The BOA
method restoring() returns TRUE if objects are being restored,
FALSE otherwise. Here is the main() function:

```
1:   // account_server3.cc
2:
3:   int main (int argc, char *argv[])
4:   {
5:     // create loader *before* BOA initialization
6:     AccountLoader loader;
7:
8:     CORBA::ORB_var orb = CORBA::ORB_init( ... );
9:     CORBA::BOA_var boa = orb->BOA_init( ... );
10:
11:    if (!boa->restoring()) {
12:      // create new objects only if not restoring
13:      new Account_impl;
14:    }
15:    boa->impl_is_ready (CORBA::ImplementationDef::_nil());
16:    orb->run();
```

```
17:    return 0;
18:  }
```

In an unshared or per-method server, you would call

```
boa->obj_is_ready (CORBA::Object::_nil(),
                   CORBA::ImplementationDef::_nil());
```

instead of `impl_is_ready()`. The sources for a complete example can be found in `demo/boa/account2`.

Sometimes it's handy to know when object saving can occur. However, you cannot be sure that these are the only occurrences of object saving:

Events that trigger the saving of objects

1. Just before a server exits, all the objects that have not been released are saved. If you do not want an object to be saved, either make its `_save_object()` method return **FALSE** or do not provide a `_save_object()` method at all. The object will then be treated as transient (i.e., it will not outlive the process in which it was created).

2. When you call `deactivate_obj()` on an object in an unshared or per-method server, the object is saved during the call to function `deactivate_obj()`. Objects saved this way will not be saved again at server exit, according to item (1).

3. When you call `deactivate_impl()` in a shared or persistent server, all currently activated objects are saved during the call to `deactivate_impl()`. Objects saved this way will not be saved again at server exit, according to item (1).

4. When you migrate an object, it is saved during the call to `change_implementation()`; see Section 4.3.6 for details. Objects saved this way will not be saved again at server exit, according to item (1).

Although the actual code for saving and restoring the state of each account object takes two lines, real-world applications often require complex code for making objects persistent. Therefore, the OMG has specified the Persistent Object Service (POS), an implementation of which is not yet provided by MICO.

4.3.6 Migrating objects

So far we have described how objects are moved between different instances of the same server. Here we explain how to move objects between two completely different servers. This is useful, for example, for replacing a server by a new version without interrupting usual business.

Recall that we augmented the account object by a management interface in Section 4.3.4. The management interface offers a method `exit()` that terminates the server when invoked. Now let's add a method `migrate()` that migrates an account object to a new server. The new server is specified through an implementation repository entry.

```
1:  // account.idl
2:  interface Account {
3:      ...
4:      void migrate (in CORBA::ImplementationDef destination);
5:  };
```

Here is the implementation of the `migrate()` method:

```
1:  #include "account.h"
2:
3:  class Account_impl : virtual public Account_skel {
4:      ...
5:  public:
6:      ...
7:      virtual void migrate (CORBA::ImplementationDef_ptr dest)
8:      {
9:          CORBA::BOA_var boa = _boa();
10:         boa->change_implementation (this, dest);
11:     }
12: };
```

The `change_implementation()` in line 10 does the whole job. It saves the object's state as described in Section 4.3.4 and tells the BOA daemon to use the new implementation from now on. See `demo/boa/account4` for an example.

4.4 POA

The BOA provides a bare minimum of functionality to server applications. As a consequence, many ORBs add custom extensions to the BOA to support more complex demands upon an object adapter, making server implementations incompatible among different ORB vendors. CORBA 2.2 added the new *Portable Object Adapter* (POA). It provides a vastly extended interface that addresses many of the unmet needs in the original BOA specification.

POA features   POA features

❏ support transparent activation of objects. Servers can export object references for not-yet-active servants that will be incarnated on demand.

❏ allow a single servant to support many object identities.

❏ allow many POAs in a single server, each governed by its own set of policies.

❏ either delegate requests for nonexistent servants to a default servant or ask a servant manager for an appropriate servant.

These features make the POA much more powerful than the BOA and should fulfill most server applications' needs. As an example, object references for some one million entries in a database can be generated, which are all implemented by a single default servant.

4.4.1 Architecture

The general idea is to have each server contain a hierarchy of POAs. Only the *root POA* is created by default; a reference to the root

Root POA   POA is obtained using the `resolve_initial_references()` operation on the ORB. New POAs can be created as children of an existing POA, each with their own set of policies.

Active object map   Each POA maintains an *active object map*, which maps all objects that have been activated in the POA to a servant. For each incoming request, the POA looks up the object reference in the active object map and tries to find the responsible servant. If

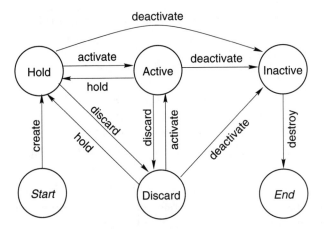

Figure 4.1
POA manager state machine

none is found, either the request is delegated to a default servant or a servant manager is invoked to activate or locate an appropriate servant.

Associated with each POA is a *POA manager* object. A POA manager can control one or many POAs. For each incoming request to an object, the POA manager's state is checked, which can be one of the following (see Figure 4.1 for a state transition diagram of the POA manager):

POA manager

Active: Requests are performed immediately.

Holding: Incoming requests are queued. This is the initial state of a POA manager; to perform requests, the POA manager must be explicitly set to the *active* state.

Discarding: Requests are discarded. Clients receive a TRANSIENT exception.

Inactive: This is the "final" state of a POA manager, which is entered prior to destruction of the associated POAs. Clients receive an OBJ_ADAPTER exception.

Before continuing, we should define more precisely a few terms that have been used freely so far.

Terminology used in conjunction with the POA

Object reference

On the client side, an object reference encapsulates the identity of a distinct abstract object. On the server side, an object reference is composed of the POA identity in which the object is realized and an *Object id* that uniquely identifies the object within the POA.

Object id

An object id is an opaque sequence of octets. Object ids can be either system generated (the POA assigns a unique id upon object activation) or user generated (the user must provide an id upon object activation). The object's object id cannot be changed throughout the object's lifetime.

In many cases, object references and object ids can be used synonymously, since an object reference is just an object id with opaque POA-added "internal" information.

Servant

A servant provides the implementation for one or more object references. In the C++ language mapping, a servant is an instance of a C++ class that inherits from the special base class `PortableServer::ServantBase`. This is true for dynamic skeleton implementations or for classes that inherit from IDL-generated skeletons.

The process of associating a servant with an object id is called *activation* and is performed using POA methods. A servant can be activated more than once (to serve many different object ids) and can be activated in many POAs. After activation, object references can be obtained using other POA methods.

Servants are not objects and do not inherit from `CORBA::Object`. It is illegal to perform operations directly upon a servant—all invocations must be routed through the ORB. In addition, memory management of servants is left entirely to the user. POAs keep only a pointer to a servant, so they must not be deleted while being activated.

Server

Server refers to a complete process in which servants exist. A server can contain one or more POAs, each of which can provide zero, one, or more active servants. Each active servant can then serve one or more object references.

4.4.2 Policies

We have already mentioned the policies that control various aspects of POA behavior. POA policies do not change over the POA's lifetime. When a new POA is created as a child of an existing POA, policies are not inherited from the parent; instead, each POA is assigned a set of default policies if not explicitly defined.

Policies influence the behavior of the POA

The root POA, described in the preceding section, has the ORB_CTRL_MODEL, TRANSIENT, UNIQUE_ID, SYSTEM_ID, RETAIN, USE_-ACTIVE_OBJECT_MAP_ONLY, and IMPLICIT_ACTIVATION policies, which are among those outlined in this section.

Thread policy

ORB_CTRL_MODEL (default)
  Invocations are performed as scheduled by the ORB. Potentially, many upcalls are performed simultaneously.

SINGLE_THREAD_MODEL
  Invocations are serialized. At most, a single upcall is performed at any time.

Non-reentrant servants should only be activated in POAs with the SINGLE_THREAD_MODEL policy. As the current version of MICO is not multithreaded, this policy is not yet evaluated.

Life span policy

TRANSIENT (default)
  Objects activated in this POA cannot outlive the server process.

PERSISTENT
  Objects can outlive the server process.

The PERSISTENT policy is not yet fully supported.

Id uniqueness policy

UNIQUE_ID (default)
  Servants can be activated at most once in this POA.

MULTIPLE_ID
> Servants can be activated more than once in this POA and can therefore serve more than one object reference.

Id assignment policy

SYSTEM_ID (default)
> Object ids are assigned by the POA upon object activation.

USER_ID
> Upon activation, each servant must be provided with a unique id by the user.

Servant retention policy

RETAIN (default)
> The POA maintains a map of active servants (the active object map).

NON_RETAIN
> The POA does not maintain an active object map.

Request processing policy

USE_ACTIVE_OBJECT_MAP_ONLY (default)
> To process an incoming request, the object reference is looked up in the active object map only. If no active servant serving the reference is found, the request is rejected, and an OBJECT_NOT_EXIST exception is returned.

USE_DEFAULT_SERVANT
> The object reference is looked up in the active object map first. If no active servant is found to serve the reference, the request is delegated to a default servant.

USE_SERVANT_MANAGER
> The object reference is looked up in the active object map first. If no active servant is found to serve the reference, a servant manager is invoked to locate or incarnate an appropriate servant.

Implicit activation policy

> IMPLICIT_ACTIVATION
>> If an inactive servant is used in a context that requires the servant to be active, the servant is implicitly activated.

> NO_IMPLICIT_ACTIVATION (default)
>> It is an error to use an inactive servant in a context that requires an active servant.

4.4.3 Example

As an example, let's write a simple POA-based server. You can find the full code in the **demo/poa/hello-1** directory in the MICO distribution. Imagine a simple IDL description in the file **hello.idl**:

```
1:  // IDL
2:  interface HelloWorld {
3:    void hello ();
4:  };
```

The first step is to invoke the IDL to C++ compiler so as to produce skeleton classes that use the POA:

```
idl --poa --no-boa hello.idl
```

IDL compiler option --poa activates code generation for the POA

The first option, **--poa**, turns on code generation for POA-based skeletons. The second option, **--no-boa**, optionally turns off code generation for the old BOA-based skeletons. Next, we rewrite the server.

```
1:  / file server.cc
2:
3:  include "hello.h"
4:
5:  lass HelloWorld_impl : virtual public POA_HelloWorld
6:
7:    public:
8:      void hello() { printf ("Hello World!\n"); };
9:  ;
10:
```

```
11:
12:  nt main( int argc, char *argv[] )
13:
14:    CORBA::ORB_var orb =
15:      CORBA::ORB_init (argc, argv, "mico-local-orb");
16:    CORBA::Object_var poaobj =
17:      orb->resolve_initial_references ("RootPOA");
18:    PortableServer::POA_var poa =
19:      PortableServer::POA::_narrow (poaobj);
20:    PortableServer::POAManager_var mgr =
21:      poa->the_POAManager();
22:
23:    HelloWorld_impl * servant = new HelloWorld_impl;
24:
25:    PortableServer::ObjectId_var oid =
26:                     poa->activate_object (servant);
27:    mgr->activate ();
28:    orb->run();
29:
30:    poa->destroy (TRUE, TRUE);
31:    delete servant;
32:    return 0;
33:
```

The object implementation does not change much with respect to a BOA-based one. The only difference is that `HelloWorld_impl` inherits no longer from the BOA-based skeleton `HelloWorld_skel`, but from the POA-based skeleton `POA_HelloWorld`.

In `main()`, we first initialize the ORB, then we obtain a reference to the root POA (lines 16–19) and to its POA manager (line 20). Then we create an instance of our server object. In line 25, the servant is activated. Since the root POA has the `SYSTEM_ID` policy, a unique object id is generated automatically and returned. At this point, clients can use the MICO binder to connect to the HelloWorld object.

However, client invocations upon the HelloWorld object are not yet processed. The POA manager for the root POA is created in the holding state, so in line 27 we transition the POA manager, and therefore the root POA, to the active state. We then enter the ORB's event loop in line 28.

In this example, `run()` never returns because we do not provide a means to shut down the ORB. If that ever happened, lines 30–31 would first destroy the root POA. Since that deactivates our active HelloWorld object, we can then safely delete the servant.

Since the root POA has the `IMPLICIT_ACTIVATION` policy, we can also use several other methods to activate the servant instead of `activate_object()`. We could, for example, use `servant_to_-reference()`, which first implicitly activates the inactive servant and then returns an object reference pointing to the servant. Or we could invoke the servant's inherited `_this` method, which also implicitly activates the servant and returns an object reference.

4.4.4 Using a servant manager

The previous example introduced the POA, but it did not demonstrate any of its abilities—the example would have been just as simple using the BOA. As a more complex example, we now consider a server that generates "virtual" object references that point to nonexistent objects. We then provide the POA with a servant manager that incarnates the objects on demand.

We continue our series of account examples. We provide the implementation for a bank object with a single "create" operation that opens a new account. However, the account object is not put into existence at that point; we just return a reference that causes activation of an account object when it is first accessed. This text shows only some code fragments; find the full code in the `demo/poa/account-2` directory.

The implementation of the account object does not differ from before. More interesting is the implementation of the bank's `create` operation:

```
1:  Account_ptr
2:  Bank_impl::create ()
3:  {
4:    CORBA::Object_var obj = mypoa->create_reference ("IDL:Account:1.0");
5:    Account_ptr aref = Account::_narrow (obj);
6:    assert (!CORBA::is_nil (aref));
7:    return aref;
8:  }
```

The create_reference() operation on the POA does not cause an activation to take place. It only creates a new object reference encapsulating information about the supported interface and a unique (system-generated) object id. This reference is then returned to the client.

Now when the client invokes an operation on the returned reference, the POA first searches its active object map but will find no servant to serve the request. We therefore implement a servant manager, which will be asked to find an appropriate implementation.

Different types of servant managers   There are two types of servant managers: A *servant activator* activates a new servant, which will be retained in the POA's active object map to serve further requests on the same object. A *servant locator* is used to locate a servant for a single invocation only; the servant will not be retained for future use. The type of servant manager depends on the POA's servant retention policy.

In our case, we use a servant activator, which will incarnate and activate a new servant whenever the account is used first. Further operations on the same object reference will use the already active servant. Since the create_reference() operation uses a unique object id each time it is called, one new servant will be incarnated for each account. This represents the BOA's unshared activation mode.

A servant activator provides two operations, which are named incarnate and etherealize. The former is called when a new servant needs to be incarnated to serve a previously unknown object id; the latter is called when the servant is deactivated (e.g., in POA shutdown) and allows the servant manager to clean up associated data.

```
1:  class AccountManager :
2:    public virtual POA_PortableServer::ServantActivator
3:  { /* declarations */ };
4:
5:  PortableServer::Servant
6:  AccountManager::incarnate (/* params */)
7:  {
8:    return new Account_impl;
9:  }
```

```
10:
11:   void
12:   AccountManager::etherealize (PortableServer::Servant s,
13:                                 /* many more params */)
14:   {
15:     delete serv;
16:   }
```

The servant activator **AccountManager** implements the so-called
POA_PortableServer::ServantActivator interface. Since servant managers are servants themselves, they must be activated like
any other servant.

The **incarnate** operation has nothing to do but to create a
new account servant. **incarnate** receives the current POA and
the requested object id as parameters, so it would be possible to
perform special initialization based on the object id that is to be
served.

etherealize is just as simple and deletes the servant. In "real
life," the servant manager would have to make sure that the servant is not in use anywhere else before deleting it. Here this is
guaranteed by our program logic.

The **main()** code is a little more extensive than before. Because
the root POA has the **USE_ACTIVE_OBJECT_MAP_ONLY** policy and
does not allow a servant manager, we must create our own POA
with the **USE_SERVANT_MANAGER** policy.

```
1:   CORBA::ORB_var orb =
2:     CORBA::ORB_init (argc, argv, "mico-local-orb");
3:   CORBA::Object_var poaobj =
4:     orb->resolve_initial_references ("RootPOA");
5:   PortableServer::POA_var poa =
6:     PortableServer::POA::_narrow (poaobj);
7:   PortableServer::POAManager_var mgr = poa->the_POAManager();
8:
9:   CORBA::PolicyList pl;
10:  pl.length(1);
11:
12:  pl[0] = poa->create_request_processing_policy (
13:    PortableServer::USE_SERVANT_MANAGER);
14:
15:  PortableServer::POA_var mypoa =
```

```
16:    poa->create_POA ("MyPOA", mgr, pl);
```

Note that we use the POA manager for the root POA when creating
the new POA. This means that the POA manager now has control
over both POAs and that changing its state affects both POAs. If
we passed NULL as the second parameter to create_POA(), a new
POA manager would be created, and we would have to change the
states of both POAs separately.

We can now register the servant manager.

```
1:    AccountManager *am = new AccountManager;
2:    PortableServer::ServantManager_var amref = am->_this ();
3:    mypoa->set_servant_manager (amref);
```

After creating an instance of our servant manager, we obtain
an object reference using the inherited _this() method. This also
implicitly activates the servant manager in the root POA.

```
1:    Bank_impl * micocash = new Bank_impl (mypoa);
2:    PortableServer::ObjectId_var oid =
3:            poa->activate_object (micocash);
4:    mgr->activate ();
5:    orb->run();
```

Now the only things left to do are to activate a bank object,
to change both POAs to the active state, and to enter the ORB's
event loop.

4.4.5   Persistent objects

Our previous examples used transient objects, which cannot outlive
the server process they were created in. If you write a server that
activates a servant and export its object reference, and then stop
and restart the server, clients will receive an exception that their
object reference has become invalid.

Persistent objects
outlive the server
they were
created in

In many cases, it is desirable to have persistent objects. A
persistent object has an infinite lifetime, not bound by the process
that implements the object. You can kill and restart the server
process, for example, to save resources while it is not needed or to
update the implementation, and the client objects do not notice as
long as the server is running whenever an invocation is performed.

An object is persistent if the servant that implements them is activated in a POA that has the PERSISTENT life span policy.

As an example, we will expand our bank to create persistent accounts. When the server goes down, we want to write the account balances to a disk file, and when the server is restarted, the balances are read back in. To accomplish this, we use a persistent POA in which to create our accounts. Using a servant manager provides us with the necessary hooks to save and restore the state: when etherealizing an account, the balance is written to disk, and when incarnating an account, we check if an appropriately named file with a balance exists.

We also make the bank itself persistent but use a different POA in which to activate the bank. Of course, we could use the account's POA for the bank, too, but then our servant manager would have to discriminate whether it is etherealizing an account or a bank: using a different POA comes more cheaply.

The implementation of the account object is the same as in the previous examples. The bank is basically the same, too. One change is that the **create** operation has been extended to activate accounts with a specific object id—we use an account's object id as the name for the balance file on disk.

We also add a **shutdown** operation to the bank interface, which is supposed to terminate the server process. This is accomplished simply by calling the ORB's shutdown method:

```
1:  void
2:  Bank_impl::shutdown (void)
3:  {
4:    orb->shutdown (TRUE);
5:  }
```

Invoking **shutdown()** on the ORB first of all causes the destruction of all object adapters. Destruction of the account's POA next causes all active objects—our accounts—to be etherealized by invoking the servant manager. Consequently, the servant manager is all we need to save and restore our state.

One problem is that the servant manager's **etherealize()** method receives a **PortableServer::Servant** value. However, we need access to the implementation's type, **Account_impl***, to query

Using STL to map servants to Account_impl

the current balance. Since CORBA does not provide narrowing for servant types, we have to find a solution on our own. Here we use an STL map, mapping the one to the other:

```
1:  class Account_impl;
2:  typedef map<PortableServer::Servant,
3:    Account_impl *,
4:    less<PortableServer::Servant> > ServantMap;
5:  ServantMap svmap;
```

When incarnating an account, we populate this map; when etherealizing the account, we can retrieve the implementation's pointer.

```
1:  PortableServer::Servant
2:  AccountManager::incarnate (/* params */)
3:  {
4:    Account_impl * account = new Account_impl;
5:    CORBA::Long amount = ... // retrieve balance from disk
6:    account->deposit (amount);
7:
8:    svmap[account] = account; // populate map
9:    return account;
10: }
11:
12: void
13: AccountManager::etherealize (PortableServer::Servant s,
14:                                    /* many more params */)
15: {
16:   ServantMap::iterator it = svmap.find (serv);
17:   Account_impl * impl = (*it).second;
18:   ... // save balance to disk
19:   svmap.erase (it);
20:   delete serv;
21: }
```

You can find the full source code in the demo/poa/account-3 directory.

Specifying the implementation name

One little bit of magic is left to do. Persistent POAs need a key—a unique "implementation name" with which to identify their objects. This name must be given using the -POAImplName command line option; otherwise, you will receive an "Invalid Policy" exception when trying to create a persistent POA.

```
./server -POAImplName Bank
```

Now we have persistent objects but still have to start up the server by hand. It would be much more convenient if the server were started automatically. This can be achieved using the MICO daemon `micod` (see Section 4.3.2).

For POA-based persistent servers, the implementation repository entry must use the "poa" activation mode, for example:

```
imr create Bank poa ./server IDL:Bank:1.0
```

The second parameter to `imr`, `Bank`, is the same implementation name as above; it must be unique within the implementation repository. If a persistent POA is in contact with the MICO daemon, object references to a persistent object, when exported from the server process, will not point directly to the server but to the MICO daemon. Whenever a request is received by `micod`, it checks if your server is running. If it is, the request is simply forwarded; otherwise, a new server is started.

Usually, the first instance of your server must be started manually for bootstrapping so that you have a chance to export object references to your persistent objects. An alternative is to use the MICO binder: the `IDL:Bank:1.0` in the preceding command line tells `micod` that `bind()` requests for this repository id can be forwarded to this server—after starting it.

With POA-based persistent objects, you can also take advantage of the "iioploc:" addressing scheme that is introduced by the interoperable naming service. Instead of using a stringified object reference, you can use a much simpler, URL-like scheme. The format for an iioploc address is `iioploc://<host>:<port>/` *IIOP URLs* `<object-key>`. `host` and `port` are as given with the `-ORBIIOPAddr` command line option, and the object key is composed of the implementation name, the POA name, and the object id, separated by slashes. So, if you start a server using

```
./server -ORBIIOPAddr inet:thishost:1234 -POAImplName MyService
```

create a persistent POA with the name "MyPOA," and activate an object using the "MyObject" object id, you could refer to that object using the IOR

```
iioploc://thishost:1234/MyService/MyPOA/MyObject
```

These iioploc addresses are understood and translated by the
`string_to_object()` method and can therefore be used wherev-
er a stringified object reference can be used.

For added convenience, if the implementation name, the POA
name, and the object id are the same, they are collapsed into a single string. An example for this is the NameService implementation,
which uses the "NameService" implementation name. The root
naming context is then activated in the "NameService" POA using
the "NameService" object id. Consequently, the NameService can
be addressed using `iioploc://<host>:<port>/NameService`. See
the interoperable naming service specification for more details.

4.4.6   Reference counting

With the POA, implementations do not inherit from `CORBA::`
`Object`. Consequently, memory management for servants is the
user's responsibility. Eventually, a servant must be deleted with
C++'s `delete` operator, and a user must know when a servant is
safe to be deleted—deleting a servant that is still known to a POA
leads to undesired results.

CORBA 2.3 addresses this problem and introduces reference
counting for servants. However, to maintain compatibility, this feature is optional and must be explicitly activated by the user. This
is done by adding `POA_PortableServer::RefCountServantBase`
as a base class of your implementation:

Reference counting
through mix-in
classes

```
1:  class HelloWorld_impl :
2:     virtual public POA_HelloWorld
3:     virtual public PortableServer::RefCountServantBase
4:  {
5:     ...
6:  }
```

This activates two new operations for your implementation,
`_add_ref()` and `_remove_ref()`. A newly constructed servant has
a reference count of one, and it is deleted automatically once its
reference count drops to zero. This way, for example, you can forget
about your servant just after it has been created and activated:

```
1:  HelloWorld_impl * hw = new HelloWorld_impl;
2:  HelloWorld_var ref = hw->_this(); // implicit activation
3:  hw->_remove_ref ();
```

During activation, the POA has increased the reference count for the servant, so you can remove your reference immediately afterward. The servant will be deleted automatically once the object is deactivated or the POA is destroyed. Note, however, that once you introduce reference counting, you must keep track of the references yourself: all POA operations that return a servant (i.e., id_to_servant()) will increase the servant's reference count. The PortableServer::ServantBase_var class is provided for automated reference counting, acting the same as CORBA::Object_var does for objects.

4.5 IDL Compiler

MICO has an IDL compiler called idl, which is briefly described in this section. The idl tool is used for translating IDL specifications to C++ as well as feeding IDL specifications into the interface repository. The tool takes its input from either a file or an interface repository and generates code for C++ or CORBA IDL. If the input is taken from a file, the idl tool can additionally feed the specification into the interface repository. The synopsis for idl is as follows:

MICO's IDL compiler translates IDL specifications to C++ stubs and skeletons

```
idl [--help] [--version] [--config] [-D<define>] [-I<path>] \
    [--no-exceptions] [--codegen-c++] [--no-codegen-c++] \
    [--codegen-idl] [--no-codegen-idl] \
    [--codegen-midl] [--no-codegen-midl] [--c++-impl] \
    [--c++-suffix=<suffix>] [--hh-suffix=<suffix>] \
    [--c++-skel] [--absolute-paths] [--emit-repoids] \
    [--do-not-query-server-for-narrow] [--feed-ir] \
    [--feed-included-defs] [--repo-id=<id>] [--name=<prefix>] \
    [--pseudo] [--any] [--typecode] \
    [--poa] [--no-poa] [--boa] [--no-boa] [--no-poa-ties] \
    [--gen-included-defs] [--gen-full-dispatcher] [<file>]
```

Command line options understood by the IDL compiler

The following gives a detailed description of all the options.

`--help`

Gives an overview of all supported command line options.

`--version`

Prints the version of MICO.

`--config`

Prints some important configuration information.

`-D<define>`

Defines a preprocessor macro. This option is equivalent to the `-D` switch of most C compilers.

`-I<path>`

Defines a search path for `#include` directives. This option is equivalent to the `-I` switch of most C compilers.

`--no-exceptions`

Tells `idl` to disable exception handling in the generated code. Code for the exception classes is still generated, but throwing exceptions will result in an error message and abort the program. This option can only be used in conjunction with `--codegen-c++`. This option is off by default.

`--codegen-c++`

Tells `idl` to generate code for C++ as defined by the IDL to C++ language mapping. The `idl` tool will generate two files, one ending in `.h` and one ending in `.cc` with the same base names. This option is the default.

`--no-codegen-c++`

Turns off the code generation for C++.

`--codegen-idl`

Turns on the code generation for CORBA IDL. The `idl` tool will generate a file that contains the IDL specification, which can again be fed into the `idl` tool. The base name of the file is specified with the `--name` option.

`--no-codegen-idl`
> Turns off the code generation of CORBA IDL. This option is the default.

`--c++-impl`
> Causes the generation of some default C++ implementation classes for all interfaces contained in the IDL specification. This option requires `--codegen-c++`.

`--c++-suffix=<suffix>`
> If `--codegen-c++` is selected, this option determines the suffix for the C++ implementation file. The default is "cc".

`--hh-suffix=<suffix>`
> If `--codegen-c++` is selected, this option determines the suffix for the C++ header file. The default is "h".

`--c++-skel`
> Generates a separate file with suffix `_skel.cc` that contains code needed only by servers (i.e., the skeletons). By default, this code is emitted in the standard C++ implementation files. This option requires `--codegen-c++`.

`--relative-paths`
> If selected, included files (via the `#include` directive) are referenced in a relative way (i.e., `#include <...>`). Furthermore, the paths of the included files are emitted relative to the include directories specified with the `-I` option.

`--emit-repoids`
> Causes emission of `#pragma` directives, which associate the repository id of each IDL construct. This option can only be used in conjunction with the option `--codegen-idl`.

`--do-not-query-server-for-narrow`
> If this option is used, the IDL compiler omits special code for all `_narrow()` methods, which inhibits the querying of remote servers at runtime. In certain circumstances, this is permissible, resulting in more efficient runtime behavior (see Section 5.6 for a detailed discussion).

`--feed-ir`

> The CORBA IDL that is specified as a command line option is fed into the interface repository. This option requires the `ird` daemon to be running.

`--feed-included-defs`

> Used only in conjunction with `--feed-ir`. If this option is used, IDL definitions located in included files are fed into the interface repository as well. The default is to feed only the definitions of the main IDL file into the IR.

`--repo-id=<id>`

> The code generation is done from the information contained in the interface repository instead of from a file. This option requires the `ird` daemon to be running. The parameter `id` is a repository identifier and must denote a CORBA module.

`--name=<prefix>`

> Controls the prefix of the filenames if a code generation is selected. This option is mandatory if the input is taken from the interface repository. If the input is taken from a file, the prefix is derived from the base name of the filename.

`--pseudo`

> Generates code for "pseudo interfaces." No stubs, skeletons, or code for marshalling data to and from **Any** variables is produced. Only supported for C++ code generation.

`--any`

> Activates support for insertion and extraction operators of user-defined IDL types for **Any**. Can only be used in conjunction with `--codegen-c++`. This option implies `--typecode`.

`--typecode`

> Generates code for typecodes of user-defined IDL types. Can only be used in conjunction with `--codegen-c++`.

`--poa`

> Turns on generation of skeleton classes based on the Portable Object Adapter (POA).

`--no-poa`

> Turns off generation of POA-based skeletons. This is the default.

`--no-poa-ties`

> When using `--poa`, this option can be used to turn off generation of tie classes if not needed.

`--boa`

> Turns on generation of skeleton classes using the Basic Object Adapter (BOA). This is the default.

`--no-boa`

> Turns off generation of BOA-based skeletons.

`--gen-included-defs`

> Generates code for IDL statements that were included using the `#include` directive.

`--gen-full-dispatcher`

> Usually, the skeleton class generated for an interface contains only the dispatcher for the operations and attributes defined in this interface. With this option, the dispatcher also includes operations and attributes inherited from all base interfaces.

Here are some examples of how to use the `idl` tool: *Examples*

`idl account.idl`

> Translates the IDL specification contained in `account.idl` according to the C++ language mapping. This generates two files in the current directory.

`idl --feed-ir account.idl`

> Same as above but the IDL specification is also fed into the interface repository.

`idl --feed-ir --no-codegen-c++ account.idl`

> Same as above but the generation of C++ stubs and skeletons is omitted.

```
idl --repo-id=IDL:Account:1.0 --no-codegen-c++
        --codegen-idl --name=out
```
Generates IDL code from the information contained in the interface repository. This requires the `ird` daemon to be running. The output is written to a file called `out.idl`.

```
idl --no-codegen-c++ --codegen-idl
        --name=p account.idl
```
Translates the IDL specification contained in `account.idl` into a semantically equivalent IDL specification in file `p.idl`. This could be useful if you want to misuse the IDL compiler as a pretty printer.

4.6 Compiler and Linker Wrappers

It can be quite complicated to compile and link MICO applications because you have to specify system-dependent compiler flags, linker flags, and libraries. This is why MICO provides you with four shell scripts:

Wrappers ease the generation of MICO applications

`mico-c++`

should be used as the C++ compiler when compiling the C++ source files of a MICO application.

`mico-ld`

should be used as the linker when linking together the `.o` files of a MICO application.

`mico-shc++`

should be used as the C++ compiler when compiling the C++ source files of a MICO dynamically loadable module. `mico-shc++` will not be available if you specified the `--disable-dynamic` option during configuration.

`mico-shld`

should be used as the linker when linking together the `.o` files of a MICO dynamically loadable module. `mico-shld` will not be available unless you specified the `--enable-dynamic` option during configuration.

The scripts can be used just like the normal compiler/linker, except that for `mico-shld` you do not specify a filename suffix for the output file because `mico-shld` will append a system-dependent shared object suffix (`.so` on most systems) to the specified output filename.

4.6.1 Examples

Let's consider building a simple MICO application that consists of two files: `account.idl` and `main.cc`. Here's how to build `account`:

```
idl account.idl
mico-c++ -I. -c account.cc -o account.o
mico-c++ -I. -c main.cc -o main.o
mico-ld account.o main.o -o account -lmico<version>
```

As a second example, consider building a dynamically loadable module and a client program that loads the module. We have three source files now: `account.idl`, `client.cc`, and `module.cc`:

```
idl account.idl
mico-shc++ -I. -c account.cc -o account.o
mico-shc++ -I. -c module.cc -o module.o
mico-shld -o module module.o account.o -lmico<version>

mico-c++ -I. -c client.cc -o client.o
mico-ld account.o client.o -o client -lmico<version>
```

Note that

❏ all files that go into the module must be compiled using the wrapper `mico-shc++` instead of `mico-c++`.

❏ `module` was specified as the output file, but `mico-shld` will generate `module.so` (the extension depends on your system).

❏ `account.o` must be linked into both the module and the client but is compiled only once using `mico-shc++`. You would expect that `account.cc` had to be compiled twice: once with `mico-c++` for use in the client and once with `mico-shc++` for use in the module. The rule is that using `mico-shc++` where `mico-c++` should be used does no harm, but not the other way around.

5 C++ Mapping

This chapter features some highlights of the IDL to C++ mapping. Sometimes we just quote facts from the CORBA standard; sometimes we describe details that are specific to MICO. Generally, we encourage using the CORBA standard as a second source. Although it certainly does not replace a good CORBA textbook, it provides invaluable details often missing in other publications.

The following sections do not cover the complete IDL to C++ mapping. Instead, we focus on some details that are often not well explained. We already assume some familiarity with the IDL to C++ mapping.

5.1 Using Strings

Strings have always been a source of confusion. The CORBA standard adopts a mapping for strings for the C++ language that is not necessarily intuitive. Bounded and unbounded strings are always mapped to char* in C++. String data is null terminated. In addition, the CORBA namespace defines a helper class String_var that contains a char* value and automatically frees the pointer when a String_var object is deallocated. When a String_var is constructed or assigned from a char*, the char* is consumed and thus the string data may no longer be accessed through it. Assignment or construction from a const char* or from another String_var causes the string to be copied.

IDL strings are mapped to char in C++*

For dynamic allocation of strings, compliant programs must use the following functions from the CORBA namespace:

```
1:  // C++
2:  namespace CORBA {
```

```
3:    char *string_alloc( ULong len );
4:    char *string_dup( const char* );
5:    void string_free( char* );
6:    ...
7:  }
```

The `string_alloc` function dynamically allocates a string or returns a null pointer if no more memory is available. It allocates `len+1` bytes so that the resulting string has enough space to hold a trailing NULL character. The `string_dup` function dynamically copies a string including the NULL character and returns a pointer to the new string. If allocation fails, a null pointer is returned. The `string_free` function deallocates a string that was allocated with `string_alloc` or `string_dup`. If a null pointer is passed to `string_free`, no action is being performed.

Helper functions have to be used for string allocation

Note that a static array of characters in C++ decays to a `char*`, so care must be taken when assigning one to a `String_var` since the `String_var` assumes the pointer points to data allocated via `string_alloc` and thus eventually attempts to `string_free` it during destruction of the `String_var` object:

```
 1:  // C++
 2:  // The following is an error since the char* should
 3:  // point to data allocated via string_alloc so it
 4:  // can be consumed
 5:  String_var s = "wrong"; // error
 6:
 7:  // The following are OK since const char* are copied,
 8:  // not consumed
 9:  const char* sp = "Hello";
10:  s = sp;
11:  s = (const char*) "World";
```

When passing strings as arguments of operations, the memory allocation functions described above should be used. See the directory `mico/test/idl/5` for some examples on how to use strings in conjunction with operations. Depending on whether strings are used as `in`, `out`, or `inout` parameters, the caller or the callee is responsible for allocation and release of the string argument. This is further explained in Section 5.9.

5.2   Untyped Values

The handling of untyped values is one of CORBA's strengths. The predefined C++ class `Any` in the namespace `CORBA` provides this support. An instance of class `Any` represents a value of an arbitrary IDL type. For each type, the class `Any` defines the overloaded operators `>>=` and `<<=`. These two operators are responsible for the insertion and extraction of the data values. The following code fragment demonstrates the usage of these operators:

```
1:   // C++
2:   CORBA::Any a;
3:
4:   // Insertion into any
5:   a <<= (CORBA::ULong) 10;
6:
7:   // Extraction from any
8:   CORBA::ULong l;
9:   a >>= l;
```

At the end of this example, the variable `l` should have the value 10. The library of MICO provides overloaded definitions of these operators for all basic data types. Some of these data types are ambiguous in the sense that they collide with other basic data types. This is true for the IDL types `boolean`, `octet`, `char`, and `string`. For each of these IDL types, CORBA prescribes a pair of supporting functions that help to disambiguate the type clashes. For the type `boolean`, for example, the usage of these supporting functions is

Helper functions are used for some basic IDL data types

```
1:   CORBA::Any a;
2:
3:   // Insertion into any
4:   a <<= CORBA::Any::from_boolean( TRUE );
5:
6:   // Extraction from any
7:   CORBA::Boolean b;
8:   a >>= CORBA::Any::to_boolean( b );
```

The usage of the other supporting functions for `octet`, `char`, and `string` is equivalent. For bounded strings, the supporting functions `from_string` and `to_string` accept an additional `long` parameter that reflects the bound.

For each type defined in an IDL specification, the IDL compiler generates an overloaded version of the operators `>>=` and `<<=` when invoked with the option `--any` (see Section 4.5). For example, given the following IDL specification:

Insertion and extraction operators are generated for each user-defined IDL type

```
1:   // IDL
2:   struct S1 {
3:     long x;
4:     char c;
5:   };
6:
7:   struct S2 {
8:     string str;
9:   };
```

the MICO IDL compiler will automatically generate appropriate definitions of `>>=` and `<<=` for the IDL types `S1` and `S2`. The following code fragment demonstrates the usage of these operators:

```
1:   void show_any( const CORBA::Any& a )
2:   {
3:     S1 s1;
4:     S2 s2;
5:
6:     if( a >>= s1 ) {
7:       cout << "Found struct S1" << endl;
8:       cout << s1.x << endl;
9:       cout << s1.c << endl;
10:    }
11:    if( a >>= s2 ) {
12:      cout << "Found struct S2" << endl;
13:      cout << s2.str << endl;
14:    }
15:  }
16:
17:  int main( int argc, char *argv[] )
18:  {
19:    //...
20:    CORBA::Any a;
21:
```

```
22:    S2 s2;
23:    s2.str = (const char *) "Hello";
24:    a <<= s2;
25:    show_any( a );
26:
27:    S1 s1;
28:    s1.x = 42;
29:    s1.c = 'C';
30:    a <<= s1;
31:    show_any( a );
32:  }
```

The main program first initializes an instance of S2 (lines 22–24) and then calls the function show_any. Function show_any tries to extract the value contained in Any. This example also demonstrates how to tell whether the extraction was successful or not. The operator >>= returns true iff the type of the value contained in Any matches the type of the variable on the right side of >>=. If Any contains something other than S1 or S2, show_any will fall through both if statements in lines 6 and 11. The complete sources for this example can be found in mico/test/idl/14.

For some IDL types, two different >>= and <<= operators are provided: a copying and a noncopying version. The copying version of the <<= operator takes a reference to the IDL type and inserts a copy of it into Any. The noncopying version takes a pointer to the IDL type and moves it into Any without making a copy. The user must not access the inserted value afterward. The copying version of the >>= operator takes a reference to the IDL type and copies the value of Any into it. The noncopying version takes a reference to a pointer to the IDL type and points it to the value in Any. The user must not free the returned value. Here are some examples:

```
1:   // IDL
2:   struct foo {
3:     long l;
4:     short s;
5:   };
6:
7:   // C++
8:   CORBA::Any a;
9:
```

```
10:   // copying <<=
11:   foo f;
12:   a <<= f;
13:
14:   // noncopying <<=
15:   foo *f = new foo;
16:   a <<= f;
17:   // do not touch 'f' here ...
18:
19:   // copying >>=
20:   foo f;
21:   a >>= f;
22:
23:   // noncopying >>=
24:   foo *f;
25:   a >>= f;
26:   // do not free 'f'
27:   // changing 'a' invalidates 'f'
```

Table 5.1 gives an overview of the operators provided for each IDL type.

5.2.1   Unknown constructed types

MICO's Any implementation offers an extended interface for type-safe insertion and extraction of constructed types that were not known at compile time. Let's look at the operators for a simple structure:

Insertion and extraction of constructed IDL types is MICO specific

```
1:   // IDL
2:   struct foo {
3:     long l;
4:     short s;
5:   };
6:
7:   // C++
8:   void operator<<= ( CORBA::Any &a, const foo &s )
9:   {
10:     a.type( _tc_foo );
11:     a.struct_put_begin();
12:     a <<= s.l;
13:     a <<= s.s;
```

IDL type	<<=		>>=	
	copying	noncopying	copying	noncopying
base type	+		+	
enum	+		+	
any	+	+	+	+
fixed	+	+	+	+
string	+	+		+
wstring	+	+		+
sequence	+	+	+	+
array	+	+		+
struct	+	+	+	+
union	+	+	+	+
interface	+	+		+
pseudo objs	+	+		+
valuetype	+	+		+

Table 5.1

Any insertion and extraction operators

```
14:     a.struct_put_end();
15:   }
16:
17:   CORBA::Boolean operator>>=( const CORBA::Any &a, foo &s )
18:   {
19:     return a.struct_get_begin() &&
20:            (a >>= s.l) &&
21:            (a >>= s.s) &&
22:            a.struct_get_end();
23:   }
```

The <<= operator tells Any the TypeCode (_tc_foo) of the structure to be inserted in line 10. Those _tc_* constants are generated by the IDL compiler. If you want to insert a constructed type that was not known at compile time, you have to get the TypeCode from somewhere else (e.g., from the interface repository) or create one using the create_*_tc() ORB methods.

After telling Any the TypeCode, the <<= operator opens a structure in line 11, shifts in the elements of struct in lines

12 and 13, and closes `struct` in line 14. While doing so, `Any` checks the correctness of the inserted items using the `TypeCode`. If it detects an error (e.g., the `TypeCode` says the first element of `struct` "foo" is a `short` and you insert a `float`), the corresponding method or `<<=` operator will return FALSE. If the structure contains another constructed type, you have to make nested calls to `struct_put_begin()` and `struct_put_end()` or use the corresponding methods for unions, exceptions, arrays, or sequences.

The `>>=` operator in lines 17–23 has the same structure as the `<<=` operator but uses `>>=` operators to extract the `struct` elements and `struct_get_begin()` and `struct_get_end()` to open and close the structure. There is no need to specify a `TypeCode` before extraction because `Any` knows it already.

5.2.2 Subtyping

Support for subtyping is MICO specific

Another feature of MICO's `Any` implementation is its subtyping support. The extraction operators of type `Any` implement the subtyping rules for recursive types as prescribed by the *Reference Model for Open Distributed Processing* (RM-ODP); see [2, 3, 4, 5] for details. The idea behind subtyping is the following: Imagine you want to call a CORBA method

```
void bar( in long x );
```

but want to pass a `short` as an argument instead of the required `long`. This should work in theory since each possible `short` value is also a `long` value, which means `short` is a subtype of `long`. More generally speaking, a type T_1 is a subtype of type T_2 if you could pass T_1 as an input parameter where T_2 is expected. This means for basic types such as `long` that a basic type T_1 is a subtype of a basic type T_2 iff the set of possible values of T_1 is a subset of the set of possible values of T_2. Figure 5.1 shows the subtype relations between CORBA's basic data types. In C++, the compiler can automatically convert types along a chain of arrows, but in a distributed CORBA application this can't be done by the compiler alone because binding between client and server is performed at runtime using a trader or a naming service. That is, the subtype checking must be done at runtime as well.

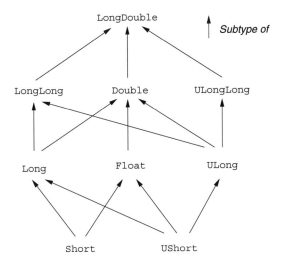

Figure 5.1
Subtype relations between basic CORBA types

In MICO, the **Any** type performs subtype checking at runtime. For example:

```
1:  // C++
2:  CORBA::Any a;
3:  a <<= (CORBA::Short) 42;
4:  ...
5:  CORBA::Double d;
6:  a >>= d;
```

will work because **Short** is a subtype of **Double**, according to Figure 5.1. But

```
1:  // C++
2:  CORBA::Any a;
3:  a <<= (CORBA::Long) 42;
4:  ...
5:  CORBA::ULong d;
6:  a >>= d;
```

will fail because **Long** is not a subtype of **Unsigned Long**. There is a special subtyping rule for structured types: A **struct** T_1 is a subtype of a **struct** T_2 iff the elements of T_2 are supertypes of the first elements of T_1. **struct S1** is, for example, a subtype of **struct S2**:

```
1:  struct S1 {
2:    short s;
3:    long l;
4:  };
5:
6:  struct S2 {
7:    long s;
8:  };
```

That is, you can put a **struct** S1 into **Any** and unpack it as a struct S2 later:

```
1:  // C++
2:  CORBA::Any a;
3:  S1 s1 = { 10, 20 };
4:  a <<= s1;
5:  ...
6:  S2 s2;
7:  a >>= s2;
```

MICO supports
recursive subtyping
　　There are similar rules for the other constructed types. MICO even goes one step further and implements recursive subtyping as prescribed by the RM-ODP. Consider the following two **struct** definitions written in CORBA IDL:

```
1:  // IDL
2:  struct ShortShortList {
3:    short x;
4:    struct Nested1 {
5:      short y;
6:      sequence<ShortShortList,1> next;
7:    } z;
8:  };
9:
10: struct LongShortList {
11:   long x;
12:   struct Nested2 {
13:     short y;
14:     sequence<LongShortList,1> next;
15:   } z;
16: };
```

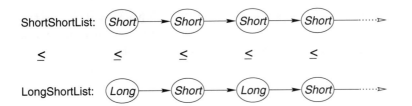

Figure 5.2
Recursive subtyping

There are two recursive **struct** definitions, called **ShortShortList** and **LongShortList**. Note that this is the only way to define recursive data types in CORBA; mutually recursive definitions are not allowed. Both **struct** definitions denote a single linked list. All the nodes of the **ShortShortList** type are of type **short**, whereas the types of the elements of the **LongShortList** alternate between the types **long** and **short**. This is depicted in Figure 5.2. According to Figure 5.1, the type **Short** is a subtype of type **Long**. Note that paired elements of the two recursive **struct** definitions are in a subtype relationship. According to the recursive subtyping rules of the RM-ODP, it follows that **ShortShortList** is a subtype of **LongLongList**. In Figure 5.2, the subtype relation is depicted through the symbol "$\leq$".

Recursive subtyping is based on a structural comparison

Using MICO's **Any** implementation, you can do the following (see also function **test_subtyping()** in file **test/dii/anytest.cc**):

```
1:  // C++
2:  ShortShortList l1;
3:  ...  // Somehow initialize l1
4:
5:  CORBA::Any a;
6:  a <<= l1;
7:
8:  LongShortList l2;
9:  a >>= l2;  // this extraction will succeed
```

5.3   Arrays

Arrays are handled somewhat awkwardly in CORBA. The C++ mapping for the declaration of an array is straightforward. Things get a bit more complicated when arrays are passed around as parameters of operations. Arrays are mapped to the corresponding

IDL arrays are mapped to C++ arrays

C++ array definition, which allows the definition of statically initialized data using the array. Assignment to an array element will release the storage associated with the old value.

```
 1:   // IDL
 2:   typedef string V[10];
 3:   typedef string M[1][2][3];
 4:
 5:   // C++
 6:   V v1; V_var v2;
 7:   M m1; M_var m2;
 8:
 9:   v1[1] = v2[1]; // free old storage, copy
10:   m1[0][1][2] = m2[0][1][2]; // free old storage, copy
```

In the preceding example, the two assignments result in the storage associated with the old value of the left side being automatically released before the value from the right side is copied.

Because arrays are mapped into regular C++ arrays, they present a problem for type-safe insertion and extraction into **Any**. To facilitate their use with the type **Any**, MICO also provides for each array type a distinct C++ type whose name consists of the array name followed by the suffix _forany. Like _var types generated by the IDL compiler, _forany types allow access to the underlying array type:

```
 1:   // IDL
 2:   typedef string V[10];
 3:
 4:   // C++
 5:   V_forany v1, v2;
 6:   v1[0] = ...;   // Initialize array
 7:
 8:   CORBA::Any any;
 9:   any <<= v1;
10:   any >>= v2;    // v1 and v2 now have identical contents
```

Array slice

Besides the _forany mapping, the CORBA standard also describes a mapping for an *array slice*. A slice of an array is an array with all the dimensions of the original but the first. Output parameters and results are handled via pointers to array slices. The array slice is named like the array itself with the suffix _slice appended. For the declaration of type M in the preceding example, the IDL compiler would generate the following type definition:

```
1:   // Generated by IDL compiler, C++
2:   typedef M M_slice[2][3];
```

Consider the following IDL specification (see also the files in directory mico/test/idl/18 of the MICO sources):

Using arrays as operation parameters

```
1:   // IDL
2:   // Note: long_arr is an array of fixed-length data type
3:   typedef long long_arr[ 10 ];
4:
5:   // Note: SS is an array of variable data type
6:   typedef string SS[ 5 ][ 4 ];
7:
8:   interface foo {
9:     SS bar( in SS x, inout SS y, out SS z, out long_arr w );
10:  };
```

The implementation of interface foo looks like this:

```
1:   class foo_impl : virtual public foo_skel
2:   {
3:     //...
4:     SS_slice* bar( const SS ss1, SS ss2, SS_slice*& ss3,
5:                                        long_arr arr )
6:     {
7:       //...
8:       ss3 = SS_alloc();
9:       SS_slice *res = SS_alloc();
10:      return res;
11:    };
12:  };
```

Note that the result value of the operation bar is a pointer to an array slice. Output parameters where the type is an array to a variable-length data type are handled by a reference to a pointer of an array slice. To facilitate memory management with array slices, the CORBA standard prescribes the usage of special functions defined with the same scope as the array type. For the array SS, the following functions will be available to a program:

Helper functions for array memory management

```
1:  // C++
2:  SS_slice *SS_alloc();
3:  SS_slice *SS_dup( const SS_slice* );
4:  void SS_free( SS_slice * );
```

The SS_alloc function dynamically allocates an array or returns a null pointer if it cannot perform the allocation. The SS_dup function dynamically allocates a new array with the same size as its array argument, copies each element of the argument array into the new array, and returns a pointer to the new array. If allocation fails, a null pointer is returned. The SS_free function deallocates an array that was allocated with SS_alloc or SS_dup. Passing a null pointer to SS_free is acceptable and results in no action being performed.

5.4   Unions

Unions and structs in the CORBA IDL allow the definition of constructed data types. Each of them is defined through a set of members. If a struct is used as an input parameter of an operation, all of its members will be transmitted, whereas for a union at most one of its members will actually be transmitted. The purpose of an IDL union is similar to that of a C union: reduction of memory usage. This is especially important in a middleware platform where less memory space for a data type also means less data to transfer over the network. You must consider carefully when to use structs or unions.

Difference between union and struct

A special problem arises with unions when they are being used as parameters of operation invocations: how does the receiving object know which of the different members holds a valid value? In order to make a distinction for this case, the IDL union is a combination of a C union and a C switch statement. Each member is clearly tagged with a value of a given discriminator type (see also mico/test/idl/21):

Union discriminator

```
1:  // IDL
2:  typedef octet Bytes[64];
3:  struct S { long len; };
4:  interface A;
```

```
 5:
 6:  union U switch (long) {
 7:    case 1: long x;
 8:    case 2: Bytes y;
 9:    case 3: string z;
10:    case 4:
11:    case 5: S w;
12:    default: A obj;
13:  };
```

In the union U as shown above, long is the discriminator type. The values following the case label must belong to this discriminator type. All integer types and enumerations are valid discriminator types. Unions map to C++ classes with access functions for the union members and the discriminant. The default union constructor does not initialize the discriminator, nor does it initialize any union members. Applications have to initialize a union before accessing it. The copy constructor and assignment operator both perform a deep copy of their parameters, with the assignment operator releasing old storage if necessary. The destructor releases all storage owned by the union. The following example helps illustrate the mapping for union types for the union U as shown above:

```
 1:  // Generated C++ code
 2:  typedef CORBA::Octet Bytes[64];
 3:  typedef CORBA::Octet Bytes_slice;
 4:  template<...> Bytes_forany;
 5:  struct S { CORBA::Long len; };
 6:  typedef ... A_ptr;
 7:
 8:  class U {
 9:    public:
10:      //...
11:      void _d( CORBA::Long );
12:      CORBA::Long _d() const;
13:
14:      void x( CORBA::Long );
15:      CORBA::Long x() const;
16:
17:      void y( Bytes );
18:      Bytes_slice *y() const;
```

```
19:
20:      void z(char*);           // free old storage, no copy
21:      void z(const char*);     // free old storage, copy
22:      void z(const String_var&); // free old storage, copy
23:      const char *z() const;
24:
25:      void w( const S & ); // deep copy
26:      const S &w() const;  // read-only access
27:      S &w();              // read-write access
28:
29:      void obj( A_ptr ); // release old objref, duplicate
30:      A_ptr obj() const; // no duplicate
31:  };
```

Discriminator
access function

The union discriminant access functions have the name _d. The leading underscore ensures that the name of the discriminator does not conflict with any other member name of the union. The _d discriminator modifier function can only be used to set the discriminant to a value within the same union member. In addition to the _d accessors, a union with an implicit default member provides a _default() member function that sets the discriminant to a legal default value. A union has an implicit default member if it does not have a default case and not all permissible values of the union discriminant are listed.

Setting the union value through an access function also sets the discriminant to the value associated with the union member. Attempting to get a value through an access function that does not match the current discriminant yields an undefined behavior. If an access function for a union member with multiple legal discriminant values is used to set the value of the discriminant, the code generated for the union by the IDL compiler chooses the value of the first case label in the union (e.g., value 4 for the member w of union U).

Based on the definition of the union U from above, the following example demonstrates the usage of the _d discriminator modifier function:

```
1:  // C++
2:  S s = ...;
3:  A_ptr a = ...;
```

```
 4:  U u;
 5:
 6:  u.w( s );    // member w selected, discriminator == 4
 7:  u._d( 4 );   // OK, member w selected
 8:  u._d( 5 );   // OK, member w selected
 9:  u._d( 1 );   // error, different member selected
10:  u.obj( a );  // member obj selected
11:  u._d( 7 );   // OK, member obj selected
12:  u._d( 1 );   // error, different member selected
```

As can be seen, the _d modifier function cannot be used to switch implicitly between different union members. The following shows an example of how the _default() member function is used:

Default member function

```
 1:  // IDL
 2:  union Z switch(boolean) {
 3:    case TRUE: short s;
 4:  };
 5:
 6:  // C++
 7:  Z z;
 8:  z._default();  // implicit default member selected
 9:  CORBA::Boolean disc = z._d(); // disc == FALSE
10:  U u;           // union U from previous example
11:  u._default();  // error, no _default() provided
```

The IDL compiler chooses a discriminator value to be used for the _default() member function, which is guaranteed not to be used for any other union member of that union. For union Z, calling the _default() member function sets the union's discriminator value to FALSE since there is no explicit default member. For union U, calling _default() causes a compilation error because U has an explicitly declared default case and thus no _default() member function. A _default() member function is only generated for unions with implicit default members.

For an array union member, the accessor returns a pointer to the array slice (see Section 5.3 on array slices). The array slice return type allows for read and write access for array members via regular subscript operators. For members of an anonymous array type, supporting typedefs for the array are generated directly into the union by the IDL compiler. For example:

Array union member

```
1:   // IDL
2:   union U switch (long) {
3:     case 1: long array[ 3 ][ 4 ];
4:   };
5:
6:   // Generated C++ code
7:   class U {
8:     public:
9:     // ...
10:    typedef long _array_slice[ 4 ];
11:    void array( long arg[ 3 ][ 4 ] );
12:    _array_slice* array();
13:  };
```

The name of the supporting array slice typedef is created by pre-
fixing an underscore and appending _slice to the union member
name. In the preceding example, the array member named _array
results in an array slice typedef called _array_slice nested in the
union class.

5.5 Interface Inheritance

The CORBA standard prescribes that IDL interfaces need to be
mapped to C++ classes for the C++ language binding. The question
is how things are handled when interface inheritance is used. MICO
offers two alternatives for implementing the skeletons when using
interface inheritance. Consider the following IDL definitions:

```
1:   interface Base {
2:     void op1();
3:   };
4:
5:   interface Derived : Base {
6:     void op2();
7:   };
```

Base is an interface and serves as a base for interface Derived.
This means that all declarations in Base are inherited to Derived.
As we have seen before, the idl tool creates stub and skeleton class-
es for each interface. The operations map to pure virtual functions,

which have to be implemented by the programmer. For the interface **Base**, this is straightforward:

```
 1:  class Base_impl : virtual public Base_skel
 2:  {
 3:  public:
 4:    Base_impl()
 5:    {
 6:    };
 7:    void op1()
 8:    {
 9:      cout << "Base::op1()" << endl;
10:    };
11:  };
```

The skeleton for **Derived** allows two different possible ways to implement the skeleton. The difference between the two is whether the implementation of **Derived** inherits the implementation of **Base** or not. Let's take a look at how this translates to lines of code. Here is the first alternative:

Alternatives for the implementation of Derived

First alternative

```
 1:  class Derived_impl :
 2:    virtual public Base_impl,
 3:    virtual public Derived_skel
 4:  {
 5:  public:
 6:    Derived_impl()
 7:    {
 8:    };
 9:    void op2()
10:    {
11:      cout << "Derived::op2()" << endl;
12:    };
13:  };
```

In the preceding code fragment, the implementation of **Derived** inherits the implementation of **Base**. Note that **Derived_impl** inherits from **Base_impl** and therefore needs only to implement op2() since op1() is already implemented in **Base_impl**.

Important: When implementing a class **X_impl** that inherits from multiple base classes, you have to ensure that the **X_skel**

constructor is the last one called. This can be accomplished by
making X_skel the rightmost entry in the inheritance list:

```
1:  class X_impl : ..., virtual public X_skel {
2:    ...
3:  };
```

Second alternative   Now comes the second alternative (note that the skeleton classes are still the same; there is no particular switch with the idl tool
where you have to decide between the two alternatives):

```
1:  class Derived_impl :
2:    virtual public Base_skel,
3:    virtual public Derived_skel
4:  {
5:  public:
6:    Derived_impl()
7:    {
8:    };
9:    void op1()
10:    {
11:      cout << "Derived::op1()" << endl;
12:    };
13:    void op2()
14:    {
15:      cout << "Derived::op2()" << endl;
16:    };
17:  };
```

Notice that Derived_impl is no longer derived from Base_impl but
rather from Base_skel. For this reason, the class Derived_impl
needs to implement the operation op2() itself. Figure 5.3 shows the
inheritance hierarchy for the classes generated by the IDL compiler
and their relationship to the classes contained in the MICO library.
Compare this with Figure 3.4 on page 32. This example can also
be found in the directory mico/test/idl/15.

5.6 Downcasting

Polymorphism   The interface inheritance described in the previous section also
induces a *polymorphism* between interfaces. This means that the

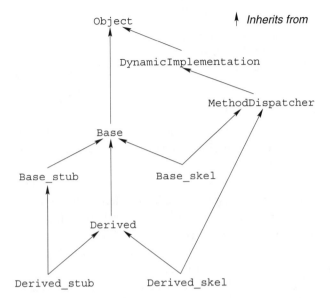

Figure 5.3
*C++ class hierarchy
for interface
inheritance*

two interfaces **Base** and **Derived** are related to each other. This relation is also known as an *IS–A* relationship or, in our example, a **Derived** is a **Base**. This means that in every context in which a reference to a **Base** is valid, the reference can be substituted by a reference to a **Derived** because a **Derived** is a **Base**.

Note that this is similar in the C++ language between a base class and its derived classes. Actually, the CORBA standard prescribes that for the C++ mapping no explicit type conversion should be necessary. Thus, with the interfaces **Base** and **Derived** from the previous section:

Upcast

```
1:  // C++
2:  Derived_ptr d = ...   // Obtain a reference to a Derived
3:  Base_ptr b = d;       // Legal, no casting necessary
```

Sometimes it is necessary to downcast a reference. The variable b in the preceding example is of type **Base_ptr**, but it actually holds a reference to a **Derived** object. It should be possible to downcast this reference back to a **Derived**. In CORBA terminology, this is called *narrowing a reference*. In the C++ mapping for CORBA IDL, each class must offer a class method called **_narrow()** that performs a type-safe downcast.

Downcast

```
1:   // C++
2:   Derived_ptr d2 = Derived::_narrow( b );
3:   if( !CORBA::is_nil( d2 ) ) {
4:      // _narrow succeeded
5:   }
```

Here the reference contained in b is downcast to a reference to a Derived object. The _narrow() method returns a NIL pointer if the downcast fails (i.e., if the object that b refers to is not derived from Base).

There is a special problem in a distributed environment when performing type-safe downcasts. Consider the following scenario: suppose there is a server that maintains references to objects implementing interface Base. Assume further that at the time this server is compiled, linked, and eventually started, the interface Derived does not exist. At a later point in time, someone decides to define a new interface Derived, which inherits from Base. What happens if the server, which is still running, is getting a reference to Derived? This should pose no problems since Derived is a Base. But since CORBA supports strong typing, from where does the server obtain this knowledge? At the time the server was compiled, linked, and started, interface Derived did not even exist.

Querying IS-A relationships at runtime

One way to solve this problem would be to stop the server, relink it with the implementation of Derived, and then get it up and running again. Sometimes, however, it is not desirable to stop the server merely because a new interface has been introduced. In that case, the only way for the server to find out if Derived is a Base holds or not is to query an object implementing Derived at runtime.

If the server receives an object reference with an unknown interface X, it queries the referenced object to see if X is a Base. The object that is queried can, of course, answer this question. Since this means a significant time overhead (a _narrow() that returns NIL will also have made a query to a remote object), the IDL compiler has a special command line option that inhibits this behavior. The code generated for _narrow() by the IDL compiler does not query remote objects if the command line option --do-not-query-server-for-narrow is used. This option should be used with caution.

5.7   Modules

In contrast to other middleware platforms, CORBA does not assign a universal unique identifier (UUID) to an interface. To avoid name clashes, CORBA offers a structured namespace, similar to the directory structure of a Unix file system. Within an IDL, a scope is defined by the keyword `module`. For example, the following IDL code excerpt defines two modules called M1 and M2 on the same level:

Modules generate a hierarchy of names

```
1:  // IDL
2:  module M1 {
3:    //...
4:    interface foo;
5:  };
6:
7:  module M2
8:  {
9:    //...
10: };
```

Module declarations can be nested, which leads to the hierarchical namespace mentioned previously. The IDL to C++ mapping offers different alternatives on how to map a module to C++. Those C++ compilers that support the namespace feature of the C++ language directly map IDL modules to C++ namespaces. Unfortunately, most C++ compilers currently have only a weak support of namespaces. In this case, the CORBA specification offers two alternatives: either do some name mangling such that a name reflects the absolute name of the IDL identifier, where the names are separated by underscores (e.g., `M1_foo`), or map an IDL module to a C++ `struct`.

Different mappings for modules

The second alternative has two drawbacks. First, without a proper support for namespaces, all names have to be referenced by their absolute names; that is, there is no C++ keyword `using` (note that this is also true for the first alternative). The second drawback has to do with the possibility of reopening CORBA modules, which allows cyclic definitions:

Reopening of modules

```
1:  // IDL
```

Figure 5.4

Dependency graph

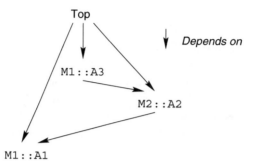

```
 2:    module M1 {
 3:      typedef char A;
 4:    };
 5:
 6:    module M2
 7:    {
 8:      typedef M1::A B;
 9:    };
10:
11:    module M1 {  // reopen module M1
12:    {
13:      typedef M2::B C;
14:    };
```

The declaration of a C++ **struct** has to occur in one location (i.e., a **struct** cannot be reopened). Mapping IDL modules to C++ structs therefore implies that reopening of modules cannot be translated to C++. However, if the C++ compiler supports namespaces, MICO's IDL compiler allows the reopening of modules. The back end of MICO's IDL compiler generates a dependency graph to compute the correct ordering of IDL definitions. Figure 5.4 shows the dependency graph for the preceding IDL specification. The correct ordering of IDL definitions is determined by doing a left-to-right, depth-first, postorder traversal of the dependency graph starting from Top.

Sometimes it is necessary to have some control over the top-level modules. For example, this is used in CORBA.h, where some definitions have to be read in one at a time. The IDL compiler inserts some #define in the generated .h file. Setting and unsetting these definitions allows the module definitions to be read in one at a time. Given the two modules M1 and M2 as before, the following C++ code fragment demonstrates how to do this:

Including top-level modules individually

```
1:  // These #includes need to be done manually if
2:  // MICO_NO_TOPLEVEL_MODULES is defined
3:  #include <CORBA.h>
4:  #include <mico/template_impl.h>
5:
6:  #define MICO_NO_TOPLEVEL_MODULES
7:
8:  // Get module M1
9:  #define MICO_MODULE_M1
10: struct M1 {
11:   #include "module.h"
11: };
12: #undef MICO_MODULE_M1
13:
14: // Get module M2
15: #define MICO_MODULE_M2
16: struct M2 {
17:   #include "module.h"
18: };
19: #undef MICO_MODULE_M2
20:
21: // Get global definitions in module.h
22: #define MICO_MODULE__GLOBAL
23: #include "module.h"
24: #undef MICO_MODULE__GLOBAL
25: #undef MICO_NO_TOPLEVEL_MODULES
```

In this example, we assume that the definitions are located in a file called module.h. First, you define MICO_NO_TOPLEVEL_MODULES, which simply means that you wish to read in the definitions yourself (line 6). For each top-level module XYZ in an IDL file, there exists a definition called MICO_MODULE_XYZ. Setting this definition will activate all declarations that belong to module XYZ (see lines 9 and 15). Do not forget to undefine these definitions after the definitions are read in (lines 12 and 19). There are some global definitions that do not belong to any module. For these definitions, there is a special **define** called MICO_MODULE__GLOBAL (see line 22; the two underscores are not a typo). The last thing we need to do is to undefine MICO_MODULE__GLOBAL and MICO_NO_TOPLEVEL_MODULES (see lines 24 and 25). This example can also be found in the directory mico/test/idl/10.

5.8   Exceptions

Limited support for exception handling

Due to the limited support for exceptions in earlier versions of the GNU C++ compiler (namely, gcc 2.7.2) MICO supports several kinds of exception handling:

1. CORBA-compliant exception handling

2. MICO-specific exception handling

3. No exception handling

Two common problems with exception handling are the following:

❏   Catching by base classes: when throwing exception X, it should be possible to catch it by specifying a base class of X in the catch clause. Some compilers (notably, gcc 2.7) do not support this.

❏   Exceptions in shared libraries: throwing an exception from a shared library into nonshared library code does not work with some compilers on some platforms (gcc 2.7, gcc 2.8, and egcs 1.x on some platforms).

Which kind of exception handling is used is determined by the capabilities of the C++ compiler and command line options passed to the configure script. By default, *CORBA-compliant exception handling* will be selected if the C++ compiler supports catching by base classes; otherwise, *MICO-specific exception handling* is selected if the compiler supports exception handling at all. If exceptions in shared libraries do not work, *no exception handling* is selected for code in shared libraries. You can enforce MICO-specific exception handling by specifying --disable-std-eh as a command line option to configure. You can disable exception handling by specifying --disable-except as a command line option to configure.

You can find out about the exception-handling support of your MICO binaries by running the IDL compiler with the `--config` command line option:

```
$ idl --config
MICO version: 2.3.1
supported CORBA version: 2.3
exceptions: CORBA compliant
modules are mapped to: namespaces
STL is: miniSTL
SSL support: no
loadable modules: yes
```

The following sections go into detail about each of the exception-handling modes supported by MICO.

5.8.1 CORBA-compliant exception handling

As the name already indicates, this exception-handling mode is conformant to the CORBA specification. You can use `throw` to throw exceptions. Exceptions are caught by specifying the exact type or one of the base types of the exception. Here are some examples:

```
 1:   // throw CORBA::UNKNOWN exception
 2:   throw CORBA::UNKNOWN();
 3:
 4:   // catch CORBA::UNKNOWN exception
 5:   try {
 6:     ...
 7:   } catch (CORBA::UNKNOWN &ex) {
 8:     ...
 9:   }
10:
11:   // catch all system exceptions (including CORBA::UNKNOWN)
12:   try {
13:     ...
14:   } catch (CORBA::SystemException &ex) {
15:     ...
16:   }
17:
18:   // catch all user exceptions (wont catch CORBA::UNKNOWN)
```

```
19:  try {
20:    ...
21:  } catch (CORBA::UserException &ex) {
22:    ...
23:  }
24:
25:  // catch all exceptions (including CORBA::UNKNOWN)
26:  try {
27:    ...
28:  } catch (CORBA::Exception &ex) {
29:    ...
30:  }
```

If an exception is thrown but not caught, MICO prints out a short description of the exception and terminates the process.

5.8.2   MICO-specific exception handling

This kind of exception handling has been invented for C++ compilers that do not support catching by base classes. For example, it is quite common to catch all system exceptions. Since catching CORBA::SystemException & does not work, you would have to write one catch clause for each of the 30 system exceptions. To work around this problem, the function mico_throw() and special _var types have been introduced.

You must not use the throw operator directly to throw an exception; instead, you should use the function mico_throw() defined in mico/throw.h, which is automatically included by IDL compiler-generated code:

```
1:  // ok
2:  mico_throw (CORBA::UNKNOWN());
3:
4:  // wrong
5:  throw CORBA::UNKNOWN();
```

will throw the CORBA system exception UNKNOWN. User-defined exceptions are thrown the same way.

Exceptions are always caught by references to the _var types. System exceptions must be caught by SystemException_var:

*System exceptions
must always be
caught using
SystemException_var*

```
 1:  // ok
 2:  try {
 3:    ...
 4:    mico_throw (CORBA::UNKNOWN());
 5:    ...
 6:  } catch (CORBA::SystemException_var &ex) {
 7:    ...
 8:  }
 9:
10:  // wrong
11:  try {
12:    ...
13:    mico_throw (CORBA::UNKNOWN());
14:    ...
15:  } catch (CORBA::UNKNOWN_var &ex) {
16:    ...
17:  }
18:
19:  // wrong
20:  try {
21:    ...
22:    mico_throw (CORBA::UNKNOWN());
23:    ...
24:  } catch (CORBA::Exception_var &ex) {
25:    ...
26:  }
```

Sometimes it is necessary to know exactly which system exception has been thrown:

```
 1:  // ok
 2:  try {
 3:    ...
 4:    mico_throw (CORBA::UNKNOWN());
 5:    ...
 6:  } catch (CORBA::SystemException_var &sys_ex) {
 7:    if (CORBA::UNKNOWN *ukn_ex =
 8:                    CORBA::UNKNOWN::_narrow (sys_ex)) {
 9:      // something1
10:    } else {
11:      // something2
12:    }
```

```
13:  }
14:
15:  // wrong
16:  try {
17:    ...
18:  } catch (CORBA::UNKNOWN_var &ukn_ex) {
19:    // something1
20:  } catch (CORBA::SystemException_var &other_ex) {
21:    // something2
22:  }
```

In contrast to system exceptions, a user exception X must be caught by X_var (i.e., not by UserException_var):

User exceptions cannot be caught with UserException

```
1:  // ok
2:  try {
3:    ...
4:    mico_throw (SomeExcept());
5:    ...
6:  } catch (SomeExcept_var &some_ex) {
7:    ...
8:  }
9:
10: // wrong
11: try {
12:   ...
13:   mico_throw (SomeExcept());
14:   ...
15: } catch (CORBA::UserException_var &usr_ex) {
16:   ...
17: }
18:
19: // wrong
20: try {
21:   ...
22:   mico_throw (SomeExcept());
23:   ...
24: } catch (CORBA::Exception_var &ex) {
25:   ...
26: }
```

It is possible to write code that works both with CORBA-compliant exception handling and MICO-specific exception handling. For this, you should follow the instructions in this section but replace _var by _catch. In MICO-specific exception-handling mode, X_catch is typedef'd to X_var; in CORBA compliant exception handling mode X_catch is typedef'd to X. Furthermore, each exception X provides an overloaded -> operator so that you can use -> to access the exception members in the catch body independent of the exception-handling mode. Here's an example:

```
1:   // throw
2:   mico_throw (CORBA::UNKNOWN());
3:
4:   // catch
5:   try {
6:     ...
7:   } catch (CORBA::SystemException_catch &ex) {
8:     cout << ex->minor() << endl;
9:   }
```

If an exception is thrown but not caught, MICO prints out a description of the exception and terminates the process.

5.8.3   No exception handling

Some C++ compilers do not properly support exceptions in shared libraries; others do not support exceptions at all. In these cases, respectively, exception handling is not available in shared libraries or not available at all.

Exception handling related C++ keywords (try, throw, catch) cannot be used in the "no exception handling" mode. mico_throw() can be used, but it only prints out a short description of the passed exception and terminates the process.

5.9   Mapping of Operation Parameters

This section describes the mapping of IDL types to operation parameter types in C++. The mapping depends on a variety of factors. One distinction is made with respect to the directional attribute of an operation parameter (i.e., in, out, inout, or a return value). Another distinction is made with respect to the type itself.

Variable and fixed-length IDL types

Besides the mapping for each possible IDL type like char or long, the CORBA standard also distinguishes between *variable* and *fixed-length* data types. A type is of variable length if it is one of the following:

1. the type any

2. a bounded or unbounded string

3. a bounded or unbounded sequence

4. an object reference

5. a struct or union with a variable-length member type

6. an array with a variable-length element type

7. a typedef to a variable-length type

Memory management policies for operation parameters

The reason for distinguishing between fixed- and variable-length data types is to allow a more flexible memory allocation scheme for actual parameters. The mapping for each IDL type is given in Table 5.2. The numbers in the table denote who needs to allocate and who needs to release memory used for the actual parameter. The policies for memory management are as follows (numbered items correspond with the numbers in Table 5.2):

1. The caller allocates storage and provides the initial value for inout parameters, and allocates the memory for out parameters, but does not need to initialize it. The callee defines the value.

2. The caller allocates storage for the object reference. If the callee wants to reassign an inout parameter, the callee first needs to call CORBA::release() to release the old storage. The caller must release out and return parameters. Object references embedded in constructed types are released automatically.

3. For out parameters, the caller allocates the storage for a C++ pointer and passes it by reference to the callee. The callee allocates storage for the out parameter. The callee is not allowed to return a null pointer. The caller must release the storage after usage.

4. The caller provides the storage for the C++ pointer as well as the string for `inout` parameters. The callee is not allowed to return a null pointer. The caller must release the string returned from an `inout` parameter using the `CORBA::string_free()` function. Memory management for strings should be done using the functions described in Section 5.1.

5. For `out` parameters, the caller allocates an array slice and passes a reference to the slice to the callee. The callee allocates an instance of the array and passes it to the caller. The caller must release the parameters using the `T_free()` helper functions generated for array slices (see Section 5.3). The callee must not return a null pointer.

6. Caller allocates storage for the valuetype instance. For `inout` parameters, the caller provides an initial value; if the callee wants to reassign the `inout` pointer value to point to a different valuetype instance, it will first call `_remove_ref` on the original input valuetype. The caller is responsible for invoking `_remove_ref` on all out and return valuetype instances.

IDL Type	in		inout		out		Return	
short	Short	1	Short&	1	Short&	1	Short	1
long	Long	1	Long&	1	Long&	1	Long	1
long long	LongLong	1	LongLong&	1	LongLong&	1	LongLong	1
u. short	UShort	1	UShort&	1	UShort&	1	UShort	1
u. long	ULong	1	ULong&	1	ULong&	1	ULong	1
u. long long	ULongLong	1	ULongLong&	1	ULongLong&	1	ULongLong	1
float	Float	1	Float&	1	Float&	1	Float	1
double	Double	1	Double&	1	Double&	1	Double	1
long double	LongDouble	1	LongDouble&	1	LongDouble&	1	LongDouble	1
boolean	Boolean	1	Boolean&	1	Boolean&	1	Boolean	1
char	Char	1	Char&	1	Char&	1	Char	1
wchar	WChar	1	WChar&	1	WChar&	1	WChar	1
octet	Octet	1	Octet&	1	Octet&	1	Octet	1
enum	enum	1	enum&	1	enum&	1	enum	1
Object ref ptr	objref_ptr	1	objref_ptr&	2	objref_ptr&	2	objref_ptr	2
struct, fix	const struct&	1	struct&	1	struct&	1	struct	1
struct, var	const struct&	1	struct&	1	struct*&	3	struct*	3
union, fix	const union&	1	union&	1	union&	1	union	1
union, var	const union&	1	union&	1	union*&	3	union*	3
string	const char*	1	char*&	4	char*&	3	char*	3
wstring	const WChar*	1	WChar*&	4	WChar*&	3	WChar*	3
sequence	const seq&	1	sequence&	1	sequence*&	3	sequence*	3
array, fix	const array	1	array	1	array	1	array slice*	5
array, var	const array	1	array	1	array slice*&	5	array slice*	5
any	const Any&	1	Any&	1	Any*&	3	Any*	3
fixed	const fixed&	1	fixed&	1	fixed&	1	fixed&	1
valuetype	valuetype*	7	valuetype*&	7	valuetype*&	7	valuetype*	7

Table 5.2

*Mapping of
operation parameters*

6   Interoperability

CORBA is an open standard that defines a specification of a middleware platform, but it does not prescribe any specific technology. Different vendors or organizations can implement their own version of the CORBA standard, just like we did with MICO. In this chapter, we show how to make MICO interoperate with other ORB implementations. The so-called IIOP provides the glue that ties together different ORB implementations. In Section 6.1, we give an overview of the parts of the CORBA standard that define interoperability. Then in Sections 6.2 and 6.3, we present a step-by-step procedure that shows how to make MICO interoperate with Orbix and VisiBroker.

6.1   GIOP and IIOP

The CORBA IDL together with a language-specific mapping defines an interface between an application and an ORB. Given an IDL specification and a language mapping, a programmer knows how to implement the client or server side of an application based only on the interface specification. In fact, the programmer does not even need to know how operation invocations are handled by the underlying ORB. We call this interface between application programs and an ORB a *horizontal interface* (see Figure 6.1).

The specification of the horizontal interface, which has been the topic for most of this document, is sufficient as long as the application uses only one ORB. But CORBA is only a specification, and different ORB vendors may make different implementation decisions, for example, for secure ORBs or real-time ORBs. One major advantage of the CORBA standard is that it also defines a *vertical interface:* the interface between two different ORBs. If ev-

Figure 6.1
*Horizontal and
vertical interfaces in
a CORBA
environment*

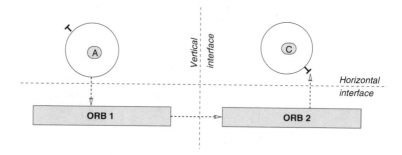

ery ORB vendor implements this interface, it should be possible to distribute an application across different ORBs, exploiting specific features of each ORB implementation.

GIOP defines a vertical interface between ORBs

The vertical interface is mostly defined by the *General Inter-ORB Protocol* (GIOP), which describes the on-the-wire representations of basic and constructed IDL types as well as message formats needed for the protocol. The design of GIOP was driven by the goal to keep it simple, scalable, and general. Furthermore, the GIOP makes some assumptions about the underlying transport protocol. The main assumptions are that the transport layer is connection oriented and reliable and models a continuous byte stream.

Mapping of GIOP to a transport protocol

The GIOP can be mapped to different transport layers meeting those assumptions. One obvious candidate is TCP, which is a de facto standard in the Internet. The *Internet Inter-ORB Protocol* (IIOP), which is part of the CORBA standard, shows how to connect different ORBs using TCP. Note that IIOP is not a completely separate protocol from GIOP, but rather an instantiation of GIOP. In fact, the transfer syntax and message formats defined in GIOP are also applicable for IIOP. The only elements added by IIOP are TCP-specific things like network addresses or connection establishment.

In the following sections, we show how to make MICO interoperate with two commercially available ORB products. With respect to Figure 6.1, we will describe a configuration where MICO is either ORB 1 or ORB 2 and the other ORB is either Orbix or VisiBroker. The vertical interface between the different ORBs is defined through IIOP.

6.2   Orbix from Iona

In this section, we demonstrate how to achieve interoperability between MICO and Orbix version 2.1c. Orbix has a proprietary communication protocol; if an Orbix object needs to communicate with
a non-Orbix object, IIOP must be selected explicitly. MICO in contrast uses IIOP by default. Iona is determined to make IIOP the
only inter-ORB protocol for future versions of Orbix.

Interoperability between MICO and Orbix 2.1c

Orbix version 2.1c comes with an example that shows how to
use IIOP between two Orbix objects. This example is a modification of the "grid" example used throughout the Orbix documentation. In the following, we show how to substitute the Orbix grid
client object by a MICO grid client object that communicates via
IIOP to the Orbix grid server.

The interface of the grid example looks like this:

```
1:  // IDL
2:  interface grid {
3:    readonly attribute short height;
4:    readonly attribute short width;
5:
6:    void set( in short n, in short m, in long value );
7:    long get( in short n, in short m );
8:  };
```

An object implementing this interface maintains a two-dimensional
grid of values of type `short`. The dimensions of the grid can be
determined at runtime via the attributes `height` and `width`. The
operations `set()` and `get()` allow the setting and retrieving of
specific elements of the grid.

The example that is shipped with Orbix version 2.1c demonstrates how to run a grid client and server using IIOP (this example
is located in the directory `corba2/demo/grid_iiop` in the Orbix
2.1c distribution). We assume that you have followed the instructions on how to run this `grid_iiop` example. If you have done so,
the persistent Orbix grid server should still be running. The server
object writes its IOR to a file called `/tmp/gridiiop.ref`.

Server running under Orbix

The implementation of a grid client using MICO is similar to
the account example in Section 3.3.2. The MICO grid client reads
the IOR, converts this into an object reference, and finally down-

*Client running
under MICO*

casts (or narrows) it to a reference of type `grid`. The client can then interact with the Orbix server object using IIOP. Here is the client object implementation for MICO (see also `demo/interop/orbix`):

```
 1: #include <iostream.h>
 2: #include <fstream.h>
 3: #include "grid.h"
 4:
 5:
 6: int main( int argc, char *argv[] )
 7: {
 8:   // ORB initialization
 9:   CORBA::ORB_var orb = ...;
10:
11:   CORBA::String_var ref;
12:
13:   ifstream istr( "/tmp/gridiiop.ref" );
14:   if( !istr ) {
15:     cerr << "error: file /tmp/gridiiop.ref not readable";
16:     exit( 1 );
17:   }
18:   char buf[ 1024 ];
19:   istr >> buf;
20:   ref = (const char *) buf;
21:
22:   CORBA::Object_var obj = orb->string_to_object( ref );
23:
24:   grid_var client = grid::_narrow( obj );
25:
26:   for( int i = 0; i < client->height(); i++ )
27:     for( int j = 0; j < client->width(); j++ )
28:       client->set( i, j, i * j );
29:
30:   for( int i = 0; i < client->height(); i++ )
31:     for( int j = 0; j < client->width(); j++ )
32:       cout << "[" << i << "," << j << "] = "
33:             << client->get( i, j ) << endl;
34: }
```

*IOR is
communicated via
a Unix file*

Lines 13–20 try to read in the IOR from a file `/tmp/gridiiop.ref`. Note that for Orbix version 2.1c this is the location where the server dumps its IOR; this could change in future versions of Orbix. Also beware that the server and client object must share the same file system, unless the file `gridiiop.ref` is copied manually to the `/tmp` directory of the host where the MICO client object is running. The IOR is converted to an object reference in line 22, and the reference is downcast to interface `grid` in line 24. Now we are ready to interact with the Orbix server object, which has to be up and running. Lines 26–28 set some values for each element of the grid. Finally, in lines 30–33, the content of the grid is retrieved and printed.

6.3 VisiBroker from Inprise

In this section, we describe how a VisiBroker object interoperates with a MICO object. This time the MICO object is the server object while the VisiBroker object plays the role of the client. To make things a bit more interesting and to show the strength of CORBA, the client object is implemented in Java. Java is particularly useful for implementing portable graphical user interfaces. For that reason, we demonstrate how to code a Java application as well as a Java applet, both of which can connect to a MICO object.

Interoperability between MICO and VisiBroker Developer for Java 3.1

6.3.1 Interoperability with Java applications

The interoperability test is based on VisiBroker Developer for Java 3.1. We use the familiar account example from Section 3.3.2 as a test. By now, it should be clear how to implement a persistent server that provides an implementation for the `Account` interface using MICO. We assume that the account object writes its IOR to a file called `account.ref`. Let us first discuss a Java application that provides the client side of the account application:

Server implemented in C++ running under MICO

```
1: import java.io.*;
2:
3: public class Client {
4:
5:    public static void main( String[] args ) {
6:       // Initialize the ORB.
7:       org.omg.CORBA.ORB orb =
8:              org.omg.CORBA.ORB.init( args, null );
```

```
 9:
10:      String ref = null;
11:      try {
12:        DataInputStream in = new DataInputStream(
13:                    new FileInputStream("account.ref"));
14:        ref = in.readLine();
15:      } catch( IOException ex ) {
16:        System.out.println("Unable to open 'account.ref'");
17:        System.exit( -1 );
18:      }
19:
20:      org.omg.CORBA.Object obj = orb.string_to_object(ref);
21:      Account account = AccountHelper.narrow( obj );
22:
23:      account.deposit( 700 );
24:      account.withdraw( 250 );
25:      System.out.println("The balance is " +
26:                                      account.balance());
27:    }
28:  }
```

Client implemented in Java running under VisiBroker

As with every Java application, the entry point is a class method called `main()` (line 5). The VisiBroker ORB is initialized in line 7. Lines 11–18 try to read the IOR of the MICO server object from a file called `account.ref`. In line 20, the IOR is turned into an object reference, which is then downcast to the correct interface type in line 21. Note that this looks very similar to the C++ version of a CORBA object client, despite some differences in the classes involved. The Java class `AccountHelper` is automatically generated by VisiBroker's IDL compiler. The remainder of the program just calls some operations, which are executed by the MICO server object.

6.3.2   Interoperability with Java applets

One of the main benefits of Java is the implementation of portable user interfaces. The new version of Netscape Communicator includes a VisiBroker ORB so that CORBA applications can be run from within this Web browser. In the remainder of this section, we show how to change the preceding Java application to an ap-

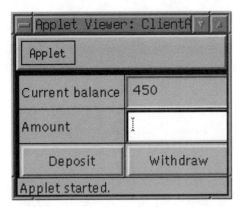

Figure 6.2
*Screen shot of the
Java applet*

plet that can be run from within Netscape Communicator. In this scenario, a MICO server object (implemented in C++) is accessed by a VisiBroker client object (implemented in Java) running as an applet and using IIOP for the communication.

As a first step, the Java application from the previous section is rewritten as a Java applet. Figure 6.2 depicts a screen shot of the graphical user interface for the account object. The current balance is always displayed in the top part of the window. An arbitrary amount can be entered in the text field below. The two buttons at the bottom of the window trigger the deposit or withdraw operation, with the amount entered in the text field as a parameter. Here is the Java source code for the account applet (the code is located in `demo/interop/visibroker`):

*Reimplementing
the client as a Java
applet*

```
1: import java.awt.*;
2:
3: public class ClientApplet extends java.applet.Applet {
4:
5:    private TextField _currBalance, _amount;
6:    private Button _deposit, _withdraw;
7:    private Account _account;
8:
9:    public void init() {
10:
11:      // This GUI uses a 3-by-2 grid of widgets.
12:      setLayout( new GridLayout( 3, 2 ) );
```

```
13:
14:     // Add the six widgets.
15:     add( new Label( "Current balance" ) );
16:     add( _currBalance = new TextField() );
17:     add( new Label( "Amount" ) );
18:     add( _amount = new TextField() );
19:     add( _deposit = new Button( "Deposit" ) );
20:     add( _withdraw = new Button( "Withdraw" ) );
21:     _currBalance.setEditable( false );
22:
23:     // Initialize the ORB (using the Applet).
24:     org.omg.CORBA.ORB orb =
25:                       org.omg.CORBA.ORB.init(this, null);
26:     // Locate the account object.
27:     String ref = getParameter( "IOR" );
28:     org.omg.CORBA.Object obj = orb.string_to_object(ref);
29:     _account = AccountHelper.narrow( obj );
30:     updateBalance();
31:   }
32:
33:   private void updateBalance() {
34:     int balance = _account.balance();
35:     _currBalance.setText( Long.toString( balance ) );
36:   }
37:
38:   public boolean action( Event ev, Object arg ) {
39:     int amount;
40:     try {
41:       amount = (int) Long.parseLong(_amount.getText());
42:       if( ev.target == _deposit ) {
43:         _account.deposit( amount );
44:       } else if( ev.target == _withdraw ) {
45:         _account.withdraw( amount );
46:       } else
47:         return false;
48:       updateBalance();
49:       return true;
50:     } catch( NumberFormatException ex ) {
51:     }
52:     return false;
53:   }
54: }
```

The entry point of the applet is method init() of class Client Applet in line 9. The applet first sets up the user interface consisting of six widgets in lines 15–21. The appearance of this applet is shown in Figure 6.2. The next step is to initialize the ORB (line 24) and to create a reference to the account object (lines 27–29).

The initialization of the applet ends by calling update Balance() in line 30, which sets the current balance of the account in the appropriate widget. This is also the first time an operation is invoked on the MICO server object (line 34). The last method action() of class ClientApplet defines the event handler for the user interface. Depending on whether the user pressed the *Deposit* button (line 42), or the *Withdraw* button (line 44) the corresponding server operations are invoked.

Buttons from the user interface trigger operations

What still needs to be explained is how the applet obtains the IOR of the server object. Java applets are not allowed to access the file system for security reasons, and even if they were, the Web browser would most certainly have no access to the file system where the server object is running. The approach taken here is to store the IOR within the HTML page, so that the Java applet can access it at runtime using the Applet::getParameter() method. The HTML page, which refers to ClientApplet.class, looks like this (see also file demo/interop/visibroker/ClientApplet. html.in):

IOR is embedded in an HTML page

```
 1: <h1>MICO - VisiBroker interoperability</h1>
 2: <hr>
 3: <center>
 4:   <applet
 5:     code=ClientApplet.class
 6:     width=210 height=100>
 7:     <param name=org.omg.CORBA.ORBClass
 8:           value=com.visigenic.vbroker.orb.ORB>
 9:     <param name=ORBdisableLocator value=true>
10:     <param name=IOR value="@IOR@">
11:     <h2>You are probably not running a Java-enabled browser.
12:     Please use a Java-enabled browser (or enable your
13:     browser for Java) to view this applet...</h2>
14:   </applet>
15: </center>
16: <hr>
```

The string @IOR@ in line 10 needs to be replaced by the actual IOR. This could be done on the Web server side after the MICO server object has initialized.

All necessary files for demonstrating the interoperability between MICO and VisiBroker are located in the directory demo/interop/visibroker. To run the demo, you need to do the following:

1. Make sure you have set the VisiBroker environment variables properly (e.g., by sourcing vbroker.sh).

2. Do make in directory demo/interop/visibroker.

3. Run server object account_svr. The server will write its IOR to a file called account.ref.

4. Run Java application with vbj Client.

5. Client should print *"The balance is 450."*

6. To run the applet version, run run_applet. The *Current balance* field should display the current balance of the account server object (450 in this case).

Notice that the shell script run_applet first patches the HTML page with the current IOR contained in the file account.ref before it runs the applet using the appletviewer. A better way to pass the IOR from the server to a client would be to use the Common Gateway Interface (CGI), but this is beyond the scope of this book.

7 Naming Service

MICO is shipped with a CORBA-compliant naming service, which is described in this chapter. MICO's naming service was implemented by Kai-Uwe Sattler (email: *kus@iti.cs.uni-magdeburg.de*) from the University of Magdeburg, Germany. Although the implementation is placed under the GNU General Public License, Sattler retains the copyright for it. We first give an overview of the naming service and then present a complete example of how to use it.

7.1 Overview

In a distributed environment, you need to address the problem of propagating references from server objects to clients. Throughout this book, we have given different solutions to this problem. The only portable and CORBA-compliant solution is to pass a stringified object reference, as described in Section 3.3.3. Note that the bind mechanism introduced in Section 3.3.3 is MICO specific and therefore not CORBA compliant.

The CORBA standard as issued by the OMG describes a *naming service* as part of the Common Object Services Specification (COSS). In order to understand this standard, we need to introduce a bit of terminology. As already pointed out in Section 3.3.3, a naming service maps names to addresses. This mapping is called a *binding* in CORBA. The addresses actually are object references or, to be more specific, instances of the IDL type `Object`.

Naming service

A name always exists relative to a *naming context*. A naming context is itself an object that can be assigned a name. This way a hierarchical namespace can be constructed. In a mathematical sense, all bindings in a CORBA environment can be modeled by a directed graph, also called a *naming graph* in CORBA terminology.

Naming context

Naming graph

Figure 7.1
A naming graph

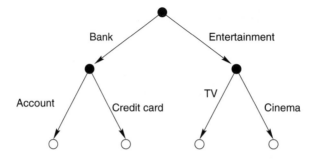

The nodes in Figure 7.1 denote objects, and the labeled vertices denote references. The black nodes are naming-context objects and the white nodes are application-specific objects.

There is no need for a unique root, but all vertices stemming from one node need to be unique. A name is always relative to a naming context; there are no absolute names in CORBA. A name is therefore an ordered sequence of components relative to a naming context. Since naming contexts are themselves objects, the naming graph can span host boundaries. The introduction of naming contexts partitions the namespace, which allows for a more flexible naming mechanism than the one introduced in Section 3.3.3.

Name consists of identifier and kind attribute

A component of a name is a tuple consisting of an *identifier attribute* and a *kind attribute* (this distinction is not shown in Figure 7.1). The purpose of the kind attribute is to distinguish between different kinds of names with the same identifier. Both identifier and kind attribute are represented in the CORBA naming service through IDL type **string** and are not interpreted by the naming service.

7.2 Name Server Daemon

Name server daemon stores name bindings

The bindings from names to objects are maintained by a name server daemon. It manages a set of naming-context objects and it answers queries from clients. There can be more than one name server daemon, which is useful when distributing the namespace over several hosts. The synopsis for the name server daemon is straightforward: **nsd**.

The name server daemon is usually run automatically by the BOA daemon. To use it, you have to run `micod`, create an entry for the naming service in the implementation repository using the `imr` tool, and pass the clients the address of the naming service using the `-ORBNamingAddr` option. A detailed example is given in Section 7.4.

7.3 Administration

MICO's implementation of a naming service comes with a little administration tool called **nsadmin**.

```
nsadmin [help | pwd | ls <binding-or-context> | cd <context> | \
        mkdir <context> | bind <binding> <stringified-IOR> | \
        rm <binding-or-context>]
```

nsadmin provides a user interface to the COSS naming service. If invoked with no command line options (except ORB-specific ones, such as `-ORBNamingAddr`), it will enter an interactive mode, show a prompt, and wait for user input. Otherwise, the command line arguments are evaluated as a command. Following is a short description of the supported commands. Context or binding names follow the syntax of Unix filenames: slashes are used to separate context names; names starting with a slash are relative to the context maintained by the name server daemon, and everything else is relative to the current context; and ".." stands for the parent context.

Commands understood by administration tool

`help`
Gives an overview of all supported commands.

`pwd`
Prints the path of the current naming context.

`ls <binding-or-context>`
If `<binding-or-context>` is a binding, this shows the associated stringified IOR. If `<binding-or-context>` is a context, this shows the contents of it. If `<binding-or-context>` is omitted, the contents of the current naming context are shown.

`cd <context>`
>   Makes `<context>` the current naming context.

`mkdir <context>`
>   Creates a new context.

`bind <binding> <stringified-IOR>`
>   Binds `<binding>` to `<stringified-IOR>`.

`rm <binding-or-context>`
>   Deletes the given binding or context. If the specified argument is a context, all of its subcontexts will also be removed.

`exit`
>   Quits `nsadmin`. This command can only be used in the interactive mode.

7.4   Example

This section provides a little example on how to make use of the naming service. The demo is located in the MICO sources under `demo/services/naming`. The server and client sides are discussed separately.

7.4.1   Server side

The example builds on the account example used throughout this book. First, we discuss the server implementation using the naming service. Notice that the implementation of the `Account` interface is the same as the one in Section 3.3.2. The full source code of the server can be found in `demo/services/naming/server.cc`.

Server implementation

```
1: #include "account.h"
2: #include <mico/naming.h>
3:
4: class Account_impl : virtual public Account_skel {
5:   // implementation unchanged
6: };
7:
8: int main( int argc, char *argv[] )
9: {
```

```
10:    CORBA::ORB_var orb = ...;
11:    CORBA::BOA_var boa = ...;
12:
13:    Account_ptr acc = new Account_impl();
14:
15:    CORBA::Object_var nsobj =
16:        orb->resolve_initial_references( "NameService" );
17:
18:    CosNaming::NamingContext_var nc =
19:        CosNaming::NamingContext::_narrow( nsobj );
20:
21:    CosNaming::Name name;
22:    name.length( 1 );
23:    name[ 0 ].id = CORBA::string_dup( "myAccount" );
24:    name[ 0 ].kind = CORBA::string_dup( "" );
25:
26:    nc->bind( name, acc );
27:
28:    boa->impl_is_ready( CORBA::ImplementationDef::_nil() );
29:
30:    return 0;
31: }
```

If you want to use the naming service, you need to include a
specific header file (line 2). The initialization and creation of a
new CORBA object is done in the usual way (lines 10–13). Note
that the implementation of the Account interface does not need to
be changed in order to use the naming service. The next step is
to obtain a reference to the naming server daemon (line 15). This
is done using the resolve_initial_references() offered by the
ORB (see Section 4.1.2 for details). This will return the reference
specified with the -ORBNamingAddr command line option. The next
step is to downcast the reference to type NamingContext (line 18).
Remember that all objects are named relative to a naming context.

The next step is to establish a new binding for the account object. We chose "myAccount" for the name, but without a specific
kind attribute. The predefined type CosNaming::Name corresponds
to an ordered sequence of tuples consisting of identifier and kind
attributes, as described earlier. We could also have chosen a com-

pound name for our object. Here is the IDL specification of Name as defined in the COSS standard:

```
1:  // IDL
2:  module CosNaming {
3:    typedef string Istring;
4:
5:    struct NameComponent {
6:      Istring id;
7:      Istring kind;
8:    };
9:    typedef sequence <NameComponent> Name;
10:  };
```

Now that we have defined a name for the account object, all that is left to do is to create a binding. This is simply done using the bind() operation of the naming-context object. The remainder of the account server implementation is as usual.

7.4.2 Client side

Once the server has created a new binding for the account object, a client can query the name server. This operation is called resolve(). The following code excerpt is taken from demo/ services/naming/client.cc of the MICO sources:

```
1:  #include "account.h"
2:  #include <mico/naming.h>
3:
4:  int main( int argc, char *argv[] )
5:  {
6:    // ORB initialization
7:    CORBA::ORB_var orb = ...;
8:    CORBA::BOA_var boa = ...;
9:
10:   CORBA::Object_var nobj =
11:       orb->resolve_initial_references( "NameService" );
12:
13:   CosNaming::NamingContext_var nc =
14:       CosNaming::NamingContext::_narrow( nobj );
15:
```

```
16:    CosNaming::Name name;
17:    name.length( 1 );
18:    name[ 0 ].id = CORBA::string_dup( "myAccount" );
19:    name[ 0 ].kind = CORBA::string_dup( "" );
20:
21:    CORBA::Object_var obj;
22:
23:    try {
24:      obj = nc->resolve( name );
25:    } catch(CosNaming::NamingContext::NotFound_var &e) {
26:      //...
27:    } catch(CosNaming::NamingContext::CannotProceed_var &e) {
28:      //...
29:    } catch(CosNaming::NamingContext::InvalidName_var &e) {
30:      //...
31:    }
32:
33:    Account_var client = Account::_narrow( obj );
34:
35:    client->deposit( 260 );
36:    client->withdraw( 10 );
37:    cout << "Balance is " << client->balance() << endl;
38:
39:    return 0;
40: }
```

Initializing of the ORB and obtaining a reference to the name server daemon are the same as for the server implementation (lines 7–14). The name, which is again of IDL type `Name`, must match the name that the server used during the creation of the binding (lines 16–19). Now we use the operation `resolve()` to query the name server for an appropriate object (line 24). Since a binding maps names to object references, we need to downcast the result of the resolve operation to type `Account` (line 33).

If an error occurs during the resolve operation, the name server throws an exception, which must be handled by the client. The exception `NotFound` indicates that the name was not found relative to the naming context (line 25). The exception `CannotProceed` indicates that the name server has given up the resolve operation for some unknown reason (line 27). Finally, the `InvalidName` ex-

Errors reported by naming service

ception denotes an invalid name, like a zero length identifier (line 29).

7.4.3   Running the example

This section shows how to run an application using MICO's naming service. We assume a simple client/server application based on the sample code of the previous two sections. The name of the executable of the server is assumed to be `server` and that of the client, in like manner, `client`. The sequence of shell commands discussed in the following are taken from the shell script `demo/services/naming/account_test` of the MICO source distribution.

Running the
example

First, we set up a `.micorc` file, which will save us some typing. Using the `-ORBImplRepoAddr` and `-ORBNamingAddr` command line options, we establish the addresses for the implementation repository and the naming service.

```
echo -ORBImplRepoAddr inet:<hostname>:12456 > ~/.micorc
echo -ORBNamingAddr inet:<hostname>:12456 >> ~/.micorc
```

Next, we have to start the BOA daemon and tell it an address to use for the IIOP protocol:

```
micod -ORBIIOPAddr inet:<hostname>:12456 &
```

Having done this, we need to register the naming service and the account server with the implementation repository (refer to Section 4.3.3 for details of the implementation repository):

```
imr create Naming shared /.../nsd \
            IDL:omg.org/CosNaming/NamingContext:1.0
imr create Account shared /.../server IDL:Account:1.0
```

Now there is a problem. Since the account server is registered as shared, it will not get started unless some client tries to connect to it. But the client will not be able to locate the account server before the server has created a binding with the naming service. We therefore need to activate the account server manually:

```
imr activate Account
```

The initialization of the account server creates a binding that enables a client to obtain a reference via the naming service. The initialization is now complete and the client can be started. You can also use the `nsadmin` tool to look at the bindings created using the `ls` command.

8   Interface Repository Browser

We have implemented a generic user interface to MICO's dynamic invocation interface. This is an add-on and not required for compiling MICO applications. The purpose of the browser is to display the contents of the interface repository in a graphical fashion. The contents of the browser can be viewed but not manipulated. The browser allows the invocation of arbitrary operations via the graphical user interface. An operation is specified with the help of a knowledge representation technique called a *conceptual graph*.

The outline of this chapter is as follows: In Section 8.1, we provide a brief introduction to the theory of conceptual graphs. In Section 8.2, we describe CORBA's dynamic invocation interface and the problems related to a generic user interface, which allows runtime access to this interface. In Section 8.3, we present the anatomy of an operation declaration as defined by the CORBA standard. In Section 8.4, we describe a generic user interface to CORBA's dynamic invocation interface based on an interactive conceptual graph editor. Finally, in Section 8.5, we show how to run the browser implemented as a Java applet using standard JDK tools (the work in this chapter has also been presented in [8]).

8.1   Conceptual Graphs

The theory of *conceptual graphs* (CGs) was developed to model the semantics of natural language (see [11]). Specifications based on conceptual graphs are therefore intuitive in the sense that there is a close relationship to the way human beings represent and organize their knowledge. From a mathematical point of view, a conceptual graph is a finite, connected, directed, bipartite graph. The nodes of the graph are either *concept* or *relation* nodes. Due to the bipartite

Knowledge representation using conceptual graphs

Figure 8.1
A simple conceptual graph with two concepts and one relation

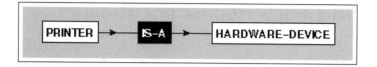

nature of the graphs, two concept nodes may only be connected via a relation node. A concept node represents either a concrete or an abstract object in the world of discourse, whereas a relation node defines a context between two or more concepts.

A sample CG is depicted in Figure 8.1. This CG consists of two concepts (white nodes) and one relation (black node), and it expresses the fact that a printer is a hardware device. The two concepts—PRINTER and HARDWARE-DEVICE—are placed in a semantical context via the binary relation IS-A. The theory of CGs defines a mapping from conceptual graphs to first-order calculus. This mapping, which is described in [11], would map the CG depicted in Figure 8.1 to the first order formula $\exists x \exists y : \text{PRINTER}(x) \land \text{HARDWARE-DEVICE}(y) \land \text{IS-A}(x, y)$. As can be seen, the variables x and y form the link between the two concepts via the predicate IS-A.

Conceptual graphs as a metanotation for arbitrary IDLs

Given a conceptual and relational catalog, you can express arbitrary knowledge. For this reason, the theory of CG represents a *knowledge representation technique*. The work done in [11] focuses on the representation of natural language. We have shown that, with a suitable conceptual and relational catalog, you can translate operational interface specifications to conceptual graphs (see [7]). We have written translators that translate arbitrary DCE and CORBA IDL specifications to CGs. Thus, we have already demonstrated that an implementation of an interface repository, which is based on such a metanotation, can be used in different middleware platforms. In the following we show how a metanotation can also be exploited for the construction of a generic user interface to CORBA's Dynamic Invocation Interface (DII).

8.2 Dynamic Invocation Interface

In this section, we present a description for CORBA's DII. For the following discussions, we refer to the interface `Account` as specified in Section 3.3.2. A client application written in C++ might, for example, use this interface in the following way:

```
1:   // Obtain a reference to an Account-object
2:   Account_ptr acc = ...;
3:
4:   acc->deposit( 100 );
5:   acc->withdraw( 20 );
6:
7:   cout << "Total balance is " << acc->balance() << endl;
```

If we assume that the current balance of the server object was 0 when the variable `acc` was bound with a reference to this object, this program fragment prints out *"Total balance is 80."* It should be clear that this program fragment requires the definition of the class `Account_ptr`. This class, which allows a type-safe access to a CORBA object implementing the interface `Account`, is generated using an IDL compiler. Thus, the type of the operational interface of the server object is known at compile time. But what if we did not know about the interface `Account` at compile time? The only possible way to access the object in this case is to use CORBA's *Dynamic Invocation Interface* (DII). This interface to an ORB offers the possibility of invoking operation calls whose signature is not known at compile time. The following code excerpt shows the usage of the DII:

Stubs allow type-safe access to CORBA objects

Accessing an object using CORBA's DII

```
1:   CORBA::Object_ptr obj = ...;
2:   CORBA::Request_ptr req = obj->_request( "deposit" );
3:   req->add_in_arg( "amount" ) <<= (CORBA::ULong) 100;
4:   req->invoke();
```

Note that the variable `obj` is of type `Object_ptr` and not `Account_ptr`. This code fragment demonstrates how to model the operation call `acc->deposit( 100 )` from the preceding code fragment. It does not require the `Account_ptr` client stub as in the last example. Despite the generic way the operation is invoked, the problem remains of how to write a generic user interface to

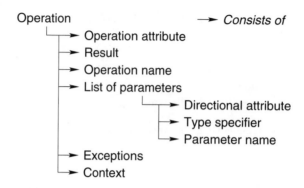

Figure 8.2
*Syntax of an
operation declaration*

access CORBA's DII. Such an interface would allow a user to invoke arbitrary operations of unknown interfaces a priori. The next section gives a brief overview of the specific details of an operation invocation.

8.3   Anatomy of an Operation Declaration

The CORBA specification describes the syntax of an *operation declaration* (see [6]). The syntax is part of the Interface Definition Language (IDL). The grammar presented in that section describes the syntax that induces a formal language. In Figure 8.2, the anatomy of an operation declaration is given, using a graphical representation of the grammar where the arrows denote "consists of"

*Building blocks of
an operation
declaration*

relations. Thus, according to the CORBA standard, an operation declaration consists of a result type, an ordered list of parameters, and so on. A parameter declaration itself consists of a directional attribute (in, out, or inout), a parameter type, and an identifier.

Note that the "graph" depicted in Figure 8.2 already has some resemblance to a conceptual graph. We propose to model the information pertinent to an operation invocation through a CG. The anatomy of an operation declaration as depicted in Figure 8.2 provides a hint as to how to accomplish this task.

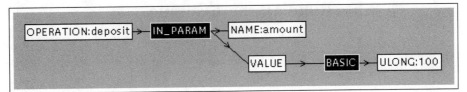

Figure 8.3
Conceptual graph representing the specification of the operation
deposit(100)

8.4   A Generic DII Interface

Consider if we had an application that allowed the browsing of an interface repository. A user would find a suitable interface at runtime and decide to invoke operations without having to write a specific client object. It would be nice to have a *generic client* that could cope with unknown operational interfaces a priori. As we have seen in Figure 8.2 and from the discussion in the previous section, an *operation invocation* consists of the following elements:

❏   a name of the operation

❏   a return type

❏   an ordered list of actual parameters

With this "anatomy" of an operation invocation, we can assemble a domain-specific conceptual and relational catalog. We have developed such a catalog, which provides the "vocabulary" to express the information needed for the specification of an operation invocation. The conceptual graph depicted in Figure 8.3 shows how to translate the operation invocation for `deposit(100)` using the DII (again, concept nodes are denoted by white rectangles and relation nodes by black rectangles). As can be seen, a metanotation based on CG provides an easily readable, formal specification of an operation invocation. It should be clear that the CG template can be extended arbitrarily to cover such specifics of the CORBA IDL as complex type definitions or sequences of arbitrary types.

Domain-specific catalog for representing an operation invocation

8.5   Running the Example

The MICO sources include an interactive conceptual graph editor
written in Java. The sources of the example are located in the
directory `mico/tools/ir-browser`. Note that you need the Java
Developer's Kit 1.1.5 as well as a parser generator for Java called
JavaCUP (see Chapter 2 for information on where to obtain these
tools). We assume that you have successfully compiled the MICO
sources contained in the directory mentioned above. Alternatively,
you can run the Java applet from your favorite WWW browser by
visiting the MICO home page.

Two files in the `ir-browser` directory are of importance for
running the example:

❏   `runproxy`: this shell script starts `diiproxy` and the interface
     repository. The IR server is then fed with some IDLs so you
     have something to browse.

❏   `dii.html`: an HTML page that makes reference to the main
     Java class `DII` implementing the interactive interface reposi-
     tory browser.

In order to run the demonstration, you first have to run the shell
script `runproxy`. You simply do this by starting it from a Unix
shell:

`./runproxy`

After this, you can load the applet by using either a Java-capable
browser or the `appletviewer` tool, which is part of the JDK. You
can run the applet by running the following command from a Unix
shell:

`appletviewer dii.html`

*Browsing through
the contents
of the IR*
Once the applet has been loaded, click on the button called
Start IR browser. A new window opens. The right side of this window shows all top-level objects contained in the interface repository. For each object, there is one icon. If you click on one of these
icons using the left mouse button, the IDL source code of that object is shown on the left side of the window. You can "enter" an

object using the right mouse button (this, of course, works only on container objects like interfaces or modules). If you click the right mouse button on an operation object, another window opens containing a conceptual graph representing this operation. You can change the input parameters of that CG before invoking it on an object.

Here is a short step-by-step tour:

1. Click with the left mouse button on the *Account* icon.

2. Click with the right mouse button on the *Account* icon.

3. Click on the *deposit* icon with the right mouse button to invoke the `deposit()` method.

4. Click on the `ULONG:0` node while holding down the shift key, enter 100 into the entry box that appears, and press return.

5. Use *Server/Invoke* to do the actual invocation.

6. Click on the *withdraw* icon with the right mouse button in the browser window to invoke the `withdraw()` method.

7. Click on the `ULONG:0` node while holding down the shift key, enter 20 into the entry box that appears, and press return.

8. Use *Server/Invoke* to do the actual invocation.

9. Click on the *withdraw* icon with the right mouse button in the browser window to invoke the `withdraw()` method.

10. Use *Server/Invoke* to do the actual invocation.

11. The rightmost node of the graph should change to `LONG:80`.

Hint: If you move the pointer over a node of the graph, the status line will show you the actions possible on this node. For example, *Shift–Button1: edit* means to press the left mouse button while holding down the shift key in order to edit the contents of the node.

Status line displays a context-sensitive help text

8.6   Using the CG Editor

The CG editor allows the insertion, editing, and removal of nodes.
The editor supports the following actions on conceptual graph
nodes:

Interactive editing
of conceptual
graphs

Left mouse button: If the working area is empty, this inserts a
new root node; otherwise, if you click on a node, you can
drag it.

Shift + left mouse button: Edit the contents of the conceptual
graph node currently pointed at.

Control + shift + left mouse button: Remove the node (and
all its descendents) currently pointed at.

Right mouse button: Bring up a context-sensitive pop-up menu.
Selecting an entry from it adds a corresponding subtree to the
node currently pointed at.

Not all of the preceding functions work on all conceptual graph
nodes. If you move the pointer over a node, the status line shows
you the actions that are possible for that node.

The order of the child nodes of a conceptual graph node is
determined by their Y-positions. The first child node is the one
with the smallest Y-position (with Y-position increasing from top
to bottom). So if you want to swap nodes A and B, just move A
below B (if A was above B before).

The *Edit* menu offers you some functions that come in handy:
New graph deletes the current graph, *Arrange graph* lays out the
nodes of the graph currently being edited, and *Linear from...*
shows you the textual representation of the conceptual graph.

9 License

This chapter contains the license conditions for MICO. All libraries are covered by the GNU Library General Public License (LGPL) version 2 or later, code generated by the IDL compiler is not copyrighted, and everything else is covered by the GNU General Public License (GPL) version 2 or later.

The idea behind this is that MICO can be used for developing commercial applications without requiring the manufacturer of the commercial application to put the application under (L)GPL. On the other hand, it is not possible to derive commercial applications from MICO without putting that application under (L)GPL.

9.1 GNU Library General Public License

TERMS AND CONDITIONS FOR COPYING,
DISTRIBUTION, AND MODIFICATION

0. This License Agreement applies to any software library which contains a notice placed by the copyright holder or other authorized party saying it may be distributed under the terms of this Library General Public License (also called "this License"). Each licensee is addressed as "you."

A "library" means a collection of software functions and/or data prepared so as to be conveniently linked with application programs (which use some of those functions and data) to form executables.

The "Library," below, refers to any such software library or work which has been distributed under these terms. A "work based on the Library" means either the Library or any derivative work under copyright law: that is to say, a work containing the Library or a portion of it, either verbatim or with modifications and/or translated straightforwardly into another language. (Hereinafter, translation is included without limitation in the term "modification.")

"Source code" for a work means the preferred form of the work for making modifications to it. For a library, complete source code means all the source code for all modules it contains, plus any associated interface definition files, plus the scripts used to control compilation and installation of the library.

Activities other than copying, distribution, and modification are not covered by this License; they are outside its scope. The act of running a program using the Library is not restricted, and output from such a program is covered only if its contents constitute a work based on the Library (independent of the use of the Library in a tool for writing it). Whether that is true depends on what the Library does and what the program that uses the Library does.

1. You may copy and distribute verbatim copies of the Library's complete source code as you receive it, in any medium, provided that you conspicuously and appropriately publish on each copy an appropriate copyright notice and disclaimer of warranty; keep intact all the notices that refer to this License and to the absence of any warranty; and distribute a copy of this License along with the Library.

   You may charge a fee for the physical act of transferring a copy, and you may at your option offer warranty protection in exchange for a fee.

2. You may modify your copy or copies of the Library or any portion of it, thus forming a work based on the Library, and copy and distribute such modifications or work under the terms of Section 1 above, provided that you also meet all of these conditions:

   a) The modified work must itself be a software library.

b) You must cause the files modified to carry prominent notices stating that you changed the files and the date of any change.

c) You must cause the whole of the work to be licensed at no charge to all third parties under the terms of this License.

d) If a facility in the modified Library refers to a function or a table of data to be supplied by an application program that uses the facility, other than as an argument passed when the facility is invoked, then you must make a good faith effort to ensure that, in the event an application does not supply such function or table, the facility still operates, and performs whatever part of its purpose remains meaningful.

(For example, a function in a library to compute square roots has a purpose that is entirely well-defined independent of the application. Therefore, Subsection 2d requires that any application-supplied function or table used by this function must be optional: if the application does not supply it, the square root function must still compute square roots.)

These requirements apply to the modified work as a whole. If identifiable sections of that work are not derived from the Library, and can be reasonably considered independent and separate works in themselves, then this License, and its terms, do not apply to those sections when you distribute them as separate works. But when you distribute the same sections as part of a whole which is a work based on the Library, the distribution of the whole must be on the terms of this License, whose permissions for other licensees extend to the entire whole, and thus to each and every part regardless of who wrote it.

Thus, it is not the intent of this section to claim rights or contest your rights to work written entirely by you; rather, the intent is to exercise the right to control the distribution of derivative or collective works based on the Library.

In addition, mere aggregation of another work not based on the Library with the Library (or with a work based on the Library) on a volume of a storage or distribution medium does not bring the other work under the scope of this License.

3. You may opt to apply the terms of the ordinary GNU General Public License instead of this License to a given copy of the Library. To do this, you must alter all the notices that refer to this License, so that they refer to the ordinary GNU General Public License, version 2, instead of to this License. (If a newer version than version 2 of the ordinary GNU General Public License has appeared, then you can specify that version instead if you wish.) Do not make any other change in these notices.

   Once this change is made in a given copy, it is irreversible for that copy, so the ordinary GNU General Public License applies to all subsequent copies and derivative works made from that copy.

   This option is useful when you wish to copy part of the code of the Library into a program that is not a library.

4. You may copy and distribute the Library (or a portion or derivative of it, under Section 2) in object code or executable form under the terms of Sections 1 and 2 above provided that you accompany it with the complete corresponding machine-readable source code, which must be distributed under the terms of Sections 1 and 2 above on a medium customarily used for software interchange.

   If distribution of object code is made by offering access to copy from a designated place, then offering equivalent access to copy the source code from the same place satisfies the requirement to distribute the source code, even though third parties are not compelled to copy the source along with the object code.

5. A program that contains no derivative of any portion of the Library, but is designed to work with the Library by being compiled or linked with it, is called a "work that uses the Library." Such a work, in isolation, is not a derivative work

of the Library, and therefore falls outside the scope of this License.

However, linking a "work that uses the Library" with the Library creates an executable that is a derivative of the Library (because it contains portions of the Library), rather than a "work that uses the Library." The executable is therefore covered by this License. Section 6 states terms for distribution of such executables.

When a "work that uses the Library" uses material from a header file that is part of the Library, the object code for the work may be a derivative work of the Library even though the source code is not. Whether this is true is especially significant if the work can be linked without the Library, or if the work is itself a library. The threshold for this to be true is not precisely defined by law.

If such an object file uses only numerical parameters, data structure layouts and accessors, and small macros and small inline functions (ten lines or less in length), then the use of the object file is unrestricted, regardless of whether it is legally a derivative work. (Executables containing this object code plus portions of the Library will still fall under Section 6.)

Otherwise, if the work is a derivative of the Library, you may distribute the object code for the work under the terms of Section 6. Any executables containing that work also fall under Section 6, whether or not they are linked directly with the Library itself.

6. As an exception to the Sections above, you may also compile or link a "work that uses the Library" with the Library to produce a work containing portions of the Library, and distribute that work under terms of your choice, provided that the terms permit modification of the work for the customer's own use and reverse engineering for debugging such modifications.

   You must give prominent notice with each copy of the work that the Library is used in it and that the Library and its use are covered by this License. You must supply a copy of this License. If the work during execution displays copyright notices, you must include the copyright notice for the Library among them, as well as a reference directing the user to the copy of this License. Also, you must do one of these things:

a) Accompany the work with the complete corresponding machine-readable source code for the Library including whatever changes were used in the work (which must be distributed under Sections 1 and 2 above); and, if the work is an executable linked with the Library, with the complete machine-readable "work that uses the Library," as object code and/or source code, so that the user can modify the Library and then relink to produce a modified executable containing the modified Library. (It is understood that the user who changes the contents of definitions files in the Library will not necessarily be able to recompile the application to use the modified definitions.)

b) Accompany the work with a written offer, valid for at least three years, to give the same user the materials specified in Subsection 6a, above, for a charge no more than the cost of performing this distribution.

c) If distribution of the work is made by offering access to copy from a designated place, offer equivalent access to copy the above specified materials from the same place.

d) Verify that the user has already received a copy of these materials or that you have already sent this user a copy.

For an executable, the required form of the "work that uses the Library" must include any data and utility programs needed for reproducing the executable from it. However, as a special exception, the source code distributed need not include anything that is normally distributed (in either source or binary form) with the major components (compiler, kernel, and so on) of the operating system on which the executable runs, unless that component itself accompanies the executable.

It may happen that this requirement contradicts the license restrictions of other proprietary libraries that do not normally accompany the operating system. Such a contradiction means you cannot use both them and the Library together in an executable that you distribute.

7. You may place library facilities that are a work based on the Library side by side in a single library together with other library facilities not covered by this License, and distribute such a combined library, provided that the separate distribution of the work based on the Library and of the other library facilities is otherwise permitted, and provided that you do these two things:

   a) Accompany the combined library with a copy of the same work based on the Library, uncombined with any other library facilities. This must be distributed under the terms of the Sections above.

   b) Give prominent notice with the combined library of the fact that part of it is a work based on the Library, and explaining where to find the accompanying uncombined form of the same work.

8. You may not copy, modify, sublicense, link with, or distribute the Library except as expressly provided under this License. Any attempt otherwise to copy, modify, sublicense, link with, or distribute the Library is void, and will automatically terminate your rights under this License. However, parties who have received copies, or rights, from you under this License will not have their licenses terminated so long as such parties remain in full compliance.

9. You are not required to accept this License, since you have not signed it. However, nothing else grants you permission to modify or distribute the Library or its derivative works. These actions are prohibited by law if you do not accept this License. Therefore, by modifying or distributing the Library (or any work based on the Library), you indicate your acceptance of this License to do so, and all its terms and conditions

for copying, distributing, or modifying the Library or works based on it.

10. Each time you redistribute the Library (or any work based on the Library), the recipient automatically receives a license from the original licensor to copy, distribute, link with, or modify the Library subject to these terms and conditions. You may not impose any further restrictions on the recipients' exercise of the rights granted herein. You are not responsible for enforcing compliance by third parties to this License.

11. If, as a consequence of a court judgment or allegation of patent infringement or for any other reason (not limited to patent issues), conditions are imposed on you (whether by court order, agreement, or otherwise) that contradict the conditions of this License, they do not excuse you from the conditions of this License. If you cannot distribute so as to satisfy simultaneously your obligations under this License and any other pertinent obligations, then as a consequence you may not distribute the Library at all. For example, if a patent license would not permit royalty-free redistribution of the Library by all those who receive copies directly or indirectly through you, then the only way you could satisfy both it and this License would be to refrain entirely from distribution of the Library.

If any portion of this section is held invalid or unenforceable under any particular circumstance, the balance of the section is intended to apply, and the section as a whole is intended to apply in other circumstances.

It is not the purpose of this section to induce you to infringe any patents or other property right claims or to contest validity of any such claims; this section has the sole purpose of protecting the integrity of the free software distribution system which is implemented by public license practices. Many people have made generous contributions to the wide range of software distributed through that system in reliance on consistent application of that system; it is up to the author/donor to decide if he or she is willing to distribute software through any other system and a licensee cannot impose that choice.

This section is intended to make thoroughly clear what is believed to be a consequence of the rest of this License.

12. If the distribution and/or use of the Library is restricted in certain countries either by patents or by copyrighted interfaces, the original copyright holder who places the Library under this License may add an explicit geographical distribution limitation excluding those countries, so that distribution is permitted only in or among countries not thus excluded. In such case, this License incorporates the limitation as if written in the body of this License.

13. The Free Software Foundation may publish revised and/or new versions of the Library General Public License from time to time. Such new versions will be similar in spirit to the present version, but may differ in detail to address new problems or concerns.

    Each version is given a distinguishing version number. If the Library specifies a version number of this License which applies to it and "any later version," you have the option of following the terms and conditions either of that version or of any later version published by the Free Software Foundation. If the Library does not specify a license version number, you may choose any version ever published by the Free Software Foundation.

14. If you wish to incorporate parts of the Library into other free programs whose distribution conditions are incompatible with these, write to the author to ask for permission. For software which is copyrighted by the Free Software Foundation, write to the Free Software Foundation; we sometimes make exceptions for this. Our decision will be guided by the two goals of preserving the free status of all derivatives of our free software and of promoting the sharing and reuse of software generally.

NO WARRANTY

15. BECAUSE THE LIBRARY IS LICENSED FREE OF
CHARGE, THERE IS NO WARRANTY FOR THE LI-
BRARY, TO THE EXTENT PERMITTED BY APPLICA-
BLE LAW. EXCEPT WHEN OTHERWISE STATED IN
WRITING THE COPYRIGHT HOLDERS AND/OR OTH-
ER PARTIES PROVIDE THE LIBRARY "AS IS"
WITHOUT WARRANTY OF ANY KIND, EITHER EX-
PRESSED OR IMPLIED, INCLUDING, BUT NOT LIMIT-
ED TO, THE IMPLIED WARRANTIES OF MERCHAN-
TABILITY AND FITNESS FOR A PARTICULAR PUR-
POSE. THE ENTIRE RISK AS TO THE QUALITY AND
PERFORMANCE OF THE LIBRARY IS WITH YOU.
SHOULD THE LIBRARY PROVE DEFECTIVE, YOU AS-
SUME THE COST OF ALL NECESSARY SERVICING,
REPAIR, OR CORRECTION.

16. IN NO EVENT UNLESS REQUIRED BY APPLICABLE
LAW OR AGREED TO IN WRITING WILL ANY COPY-
RIGHT HOLDER, OR ANY OTHER PARTY WHO MAY
MODIFY AND/OR REDISTRIBUTE THE LIBRARY AS
PERMITTED ABOVE, BE LIABLE TO YOU FOR DAM-
AGES, INCLUDING ANY GENERAL, SPECIAL, INCI-
DENTAL, OR CONSEQUENTIAL DAMAGES ARISING
OUT OF THE USE OR INABILITY TO USE THE LI-
BRARY (INCLUDING BUT NOT LIMITED TO LOSS OF
DATA OR DATA BEING RENDERED INACCURATE OR
LOSSES SUSTAINED BY YOU OR THIRD PARTIES OR
A FAILURE OF THE LIBRARY TO OPERATE WITH
ANY OTHER SOFTWARE), EVEN IF SUCH HOLDER
OR OTHER PARTY HAS BEEN ADVISED OF THE POS-
SIBILITY OF SUCH DAMAGES.

END OF TERMS AND CONDITIONS

9.2 GNU General Public License

TERMS AND CONDITIONS FOR COPYING,
DISTRIBUTION, AND MODIFICATION

0. This License applies to any program or other work which contains a notice placed by the copyright holder saying it may be distributed under the terms of this General Public License. The "Program," below, refers to any such program or work, and a "work based on the Program" means either the Program or any derivative work under copyright law: that is to say, a work containing the Program or a portion of it, either verbatim or with modifications and/or translated into another language. (Hereinafter, translation is included without limitation in the term "modification.") Each licensee is addressed as "you."

   Activities other than copying, distribution, and modification are not covered by this License; they are outside its scope. The act of running the Program is not restricted, and the output from the Program is covered only if its contents constitute a work based on the Program (independent of having been made by running the Program). Whether that is true depends on what the Program does.

1. You may copy and distribute verbatim copies of the Program's source code as you receive it, in any medium, provided that you conspicuously and appropriately publish on each copy an appropriate copyright notice and disclaimer of warranty; keep intact all the notices that refer to this License and to the absence of any warranty; and give any other recipients of the Program a copy of this License along with the Program.

   You may charge a fee for the physical act of transferring a copy, and you may at your option offer warranty protection in exchange for a fee.

2. You may modify your copy or copies of the Program or any portion of it, thus forming a work based on the Program, and copy and distribute such modifications or work under

the terms of Section 1 above, provided that you also meet all of these conditions:

a) You must cause the modified files to carry prominent notices stating that you changed the files and the date of any change.

b) You must cause any work that you distribute or publish, that in whole or in part contains or is derived from the Program or any part thereof, to be licensed as a whole at no charge to all third parties under the terms of this License.

c) If the modified program normally reads commands interactively when run, you must cause it, when started running for such interactive use in the most ordinary way, to print or display an announcement including an appropriate copyright notice and a notice that there is no warranty (or else, saying that you provide a warranty) and that users may redistribute the program under these conditions, and telling the user how to view a copy of this License. (Exception: If the Program itself is interactive but does not normally print such an announcement, your work based on the Program is not required to print an announcement.)

These requirements apply to the modified work as a whole. If identifiable sections of that work are not derived from the Program, and can be reasonably considered independent and separate works in themselves, then this License, and its terms, do not apply to those sections when you distribute them as separate works. But when you distribute the same sections as part of a whole which is a work based on the Program, the distribution of the whole must be on the terms of this License, whose permissions for other licensees extend to the entire whole, and thus to each and every part regardless of who wrote it.

Thus, it is not the intent of this section to claim rights or contest your rights to work written entirely by you; rather, the intent is to exercise the right to control the distribution of derivative or collective works based on the Program.

In addition, mere aggregation of another work not based on the Program with the Program (or with a work based on the Program) on a volume of a storage or distribution medium does not bring the other work under the scope of this License.

3. You may copy and distribute the Program (or a work based on it, under Section 2) in object code or executable form under the terms of Sections 1 and 2 above provided that you also do one of the following:

   a) Accompany it with the complete corresponding machine-readable source code, which must be distributed under the terms of Sections 1 and 2 above on a medium customarily used for software interchange; or,

   b) Accompany it with a written offer, valid for at least three years, to give any third party, for a charge no more than your cost of physically performing source distribution, a complete machine-readable copy of the corresponding source code, to be distributed under the terms of Sections 1 and 2 above on a medium customarily used for software interchange; or,

   c) Accompany it with the information you received as to the offer to distribute corresponding source code. (This alternative is allowed only for noncommercial distribution and only if you received the program in object code or executable form with such an offer, in accord with Subsection b above.)

The source code for a work means the preferred form of the work for making modifications to it. For an executable work, complete source code means all the source code for all modules it contains, plus any associated interface definition files, plus the scripts used to control compilation and installation of the executable. However, as a special exception, the source code distributed need not include anything that is normally distributed (in either source or binary form) with the major components (compiler, kernel, and so on) of the operating system on which the executable runs, unless that component itself accompanies the executable.

If distribution of executable or object code is made by offering access to copy from a designated place, then offering equivalent access to copy the source code from the same place counts as distribution of the source code, even though third parties are not compelled to copy the source along with the object code.

4. You may not copy, modify, sublicense, or distribute the Program except as expressly provided under this License. Any attempt otherwise to copy, modify, sublicense, or distribute the Program is void, and will automatically terminate your rights under this License. However, parties who have received copies, or rights, from you under this License will not have their licenses terminated so long as such parties remain in full compliance.

5. You are not required to accept this License, since you have not signed it. However, nothing else grants you permission to modify or distribute the Program or its derivative works. These actions are prohibited by law if you do not accept this License. Therefore, by modifying or distributing the Program (or any work based on the Program), you indicate your acceptance of this License to do so, and all its terms and conditions for copying, distributing, or modifying the Program or works based on it.

6. Each time you redistribute the Program (or any work based on the Program), the recipient automatically receives a license from the original licensor to copy, distribute, or modify the Program subject to these terms and conditions. You may not impose any further restrictions on the recipients' exercise of the rights granted herein. You are not responsible for enforcing compliance by third parties to this License.

7. If, as a consequence of a court judgment or allegation of patent infringement or for any other reason (not limited to patent issues), conditions are imposed on you (whether by

court order, agreement, or otherwise) that contradict the conditions of this License, they do not excuse you from the conditions of this License. If you cannot distribute so as to satisfy simultaneously your obligations under this License and any other pertinent obligations, then as a consequence you may not distribute the Program at all. For example, if a patent license would not permit royalty-free redistribution of the Program by all those who receive copies directly or indirectly through you, then the only way you could satisfy both it and this License would be to refrain entirely from distribution of the Program.

If any portion of this section is held invalid or unenforceable under any particular circumstance, the balance of the section is intended to apply and the section as a whole is intended to apply in other circumstances.

It is not the purpose of this section to induce you to infringe any patents or other property right claims or to contest validity of any such claims; this section has the sole purpose of protecting the integrity of the free software distribution system, which is implemented by public license practices. Many people have made generous contributions to the wide range of software distributed through that system in reliance on consistent application of that system; it is up to the author/donor to decide if he or she is willing to distribute software through any other system and a licensee cannot impose that choice.

This section is intended to make thoroughly clear what is believed to be a consequence of the rest of this License.

8. If the distribution and/or use of the Program is restricted in certain countries either by patents or by copyrighted interfaces, the original copyright holder who places the Program under this License may add an explicit geographical distribution limitation excluding those countries, so that distribution is permitted only in or among countries not thus excluded. In such case, this License incorporates the limitation as if written in the body of this License.

9. The Free Software Foundation may publish revised and/or new versions of the General Public License from time to time. Such new versions will be similar in spirit to the present version, but may differ in detail to address new problems or concerns.

Each version is given a distinguishing version number. If the Program specifies a version number of this License which applies to it and "any later version," you have the option of following the terms and conditions either of that version or of any later version published by the Free Software Foundation. If the Program does not specify a version number of this License, you may choose any version ever published by the Free Software Foundation.

10. If you wish to incorporate parts of the Program into other free programs whose distribution conditions are different, write to the author to ask for permission. For software which is copyrighted by the Free Software Foundation, write to the Free Software Foundation; we sometimes make exceptions for this. Our decision will be guided by the two goals of preserving the free status of all derivatives of our free software and of promoting the sharing and reuse of software generally.

NO WARRANTY

11. BECAUSE THE PROGRAM IS LICENSED FREE OF CHARGE, THERE IS NO WARRANTY FOR THE PROGRAM, TO THE EXTENT PERMITTED BY APPLICABLE LAW. EXCEPT WHEN OTHERWISE STATED IN WRITING THE COPYRIGHT HOLDERS AND/OR OTHER PARTIES PROVIDE THE PROGRAM "AS IS" WITHOUT WARRANTY OF ANY KIND, EITHER EXPRESSED OR IMPLIED, INCLUDING, BUT NOT LIMITED TO, THE IMPLIED WARRANTIES OF MERCHANTABILITY AND FITNESS FOR A PARTICULAR PURPOSE. THE ENTIRE RISK AS TO THE QUALITY AND PERFORMANCE OF THE PROGRAM IS WITH YOU. SHOULD THE PROGRAM PROVE DEFECTIVE, YOU

ASSUME THE COST OF ALL NECESSARY SERVICING, REPAIR, OR CORRECTION.

12. IN NO EVENT UNLESS REQUIRED BY APPLICABLE LAW OR AGREED TO IN WRITING WILL ANY COPYRIGHT HOLDER, OR ANY OTHER PARTY WHO MAY MODIFY AND/OR REDISTRIBUTE THE PROGRAM AS PERMITTED ABOVE, BE LIABLE TO YOU FOR DAMAGES, INCLUDING ANY GENERAL, SPECIAL, INCIDENTAL, OR CONSEQUENTIAL DAMAGES ARISING OUT OF THE USE OR INABILITY TO USE THE PROGRAM (INCLUDING BUT NOT LIMITED TO LOSS OF DATA OR DATA BEING RENDERED INACCURATE OR LOSSES SUSTAINED BY YOU OR THIRD PARTIES OR A FAILURE OF THE PROGRAM TO OPERATE WITH ANY OTHER PROGRAMS), EVEN IF SUCH HOLDER OR OTHER PARTY HAS BEEN ADVISED OF THE POSSIBILITY OF SUCH DAMAGES.

END OF TERMS AND CONDITIONS

A   Sample Programs

Many good books have been written about CORBA. Most of them include some sample programs that demonstrate the usage of COR-BA. One possible use of MICO is to get hands-on experience with the CORBA technology without paying a lot of money for a commercial product. To make life a bit easier, we provide ported versions for MICO of the sample programs contained in three prominent CORBA books: *CORBA 3: Fundamentals and Programming* by J. Siegel, *CORBA 2.0—Eine praktische Einführung für C++ und Java* by J.P. Redlich, and *Advanced CORBA Programming with C++* by M. Henning and S. Vinoski.

A.1   Siegel's Examples

The directory `$(MICO_HOME)/doc/examples/siegel` contains the source code of the examples given in Siegel's book *CORBA 3: Fundamentals and Programming* (see [10]). The source code was graciously provided by Jon Siegel (email: *siegel@omg.org*). Simply type `make` in this directory to compile the example. You can make use of MICO's POA daemon to launch the application. The shell script `run_demo`, which is also contained in the same directory, starts the demo and enters the interactive client described in Siegel's book.

A.2   Redlich's Examples

J.P. Redlich, the author of the book *CORBA 2.0—Eine praktische Einführung für C++ und Java* (see [9]), has ported various programs from his book to MICO and made them available. These files are located in the directory $(MICO_HOME)/doc/examples/redlich/, where the environment variable $(MICO_HOME) denotes the directory where you installed MICO on your system. The author has placed his demo programs under the GNU General Public License. For that reason, we were able to include the complete sources of these programs with this distribution and there is no need to apply any diffs in this case. Refer to J.P. Redlich's book for explanations of the programs. In order to compile them, you simply need to run make from the directory $(MICO_HOME)/doc/examples/redlich/.

A.3   Henning's and Vinoski's Examples

The book by M. Henning and S. Vinoski, *Advanced CORBA Programming with C++* (see [1]), has become very popular in the CORBA community. It provides a profound knowledge on CORBA. It does not merely reiterate facts from the CORBA specification, but provides explanations as to why things have been specified as they have. We strongly recommend this book as a valuable addition for C++ programmers who want to learn CORBA. The sample programs of this book are contained in the directory $(MICO_HOME)/doc/examples/henning/ of the MICO distribution.

B Frequently Asked Questions

A lot of traffic on our mailing list (see Section 1.3) is concerned with problems people encounter while installing and using MICO. Therefore we have collected frequently asked questions (also known as FAQs) and their answers. If you encounter a problem, first check the FAQs to see if there is a solution. If your problem is not listed, please send your inquiry to the mailing list. Include a detailed description of your problem along with

- the MICO version

- the operating system you are running on

- the hardware you are running on

- the compiler type and version you are using

- a stack trace

To get a stack trace, run the offending program in the debugger:

```
gdb <prog>
(gdb) run <args>
program got signal ???
(gdb) backtrace
```

and include the output in your mail.

Q: *During compilation, gcc 2.7.2.x aborts with an "internal compiler error." What is going wrong?*

A: Some Linux distributions (notably, Suse Linux 5 and Red-Hat) shipped broken gcc binaries. You have to recompile gcc 2.7.2.x, or better yet, install egcs 1.x or gcc 2.8.x.

Q: *Compilation aborts with a "virtual memory exhausted" error. What can I do?*

A: Add more swap space. Under Linux, you can simply create a swap file:

```
su
dd if=/dev/zero of=/tmp/swapfile bs=1024 \
    count=64000
mkswap /tmp/swapfile
swapon /tmp/swapfile
```

There are similar ways for other Unix flavors. Ask your sys admin. If for some reason you cannot add more swap space, try turning off optimization by rerunning configure:

```
./configure --disable-optimize
```

Q: *I use Cygnus CDK. gcc aborts with a "virtual memory exhausted" error. How can this be fixed?*

A: There seems to be a bug in Cygnus CDK beta 19 that prevents gcc from using swap space. One workaround is to disable optimization by rerunning configure:

```
./configure --disable-optimize
```

Q: *I use Cygnus CDK. MICO applications hang forever.*

A: Please refer to Section 2.1.1.

Q: *I use Cygnus CDK. Exception handling does not work.*

A: Please refer to Section 2.1.1.

Q: *I configured for namespace support, but MICO doesn't compile.*

A: Earlier versions of gcc and egcs (up to gcc 2.8.x and egcs 1.0.x) have very limited namespace support. The tests configure uses to check for working namespaces pass, but MICO itself fails to compile. Rerun configure without `--enable-namespace`.

Q: *I use Visual C++. Compilation aborts with an error.*

A: Please refer to Section 2.1.1.

Q: *I try to compile MICO on HP-UX using gcc 2.7.2. Everything compiles fine, but linking fails.*

A: Please refer to Section 2.1.2.

Q: *I'm using egcs 1.x. If I turn off MiniSTL, compilation aborts with*

```
/usr/ccs/bin/as: error: can't compute value of
an expression involving an external symbol
```

A: This is a bug in egcs, which can be worked around by using -g:

```
./configure --enable-debug
```

Q: *All MICO programs crash. Why?*

A: There is no easy answer. Often this is caused by linking
with wrong versions of system libraries. For example, people
often install egcs as a second compiler on their system and set
PATH such that egcs will be used. But that is not enough:
you have to make sure that egcs's C++ libraries (especially
libstdc++) will be linked in. One way to make MICO use egcs
installed in `/usr/local/egcs` is

```
export PATH=/usr/local/egcs/bin:$PATH
export CXXFLAGS=-L/usr/local/egcs/lib
export LD_LIBRARY_PATH=/usr/local/egcs/lib:\
  $LD_LIBRARY_PATH
./configure
```

If that does not help, you probably found a bug in MICO.
Send an inquiry to the mailing list (see Section 1.3) containing
a detailed description of the problem.

Q: *After creating implementation repository entries with* imr
create, imr list *does not show the newly created entries.
What is going wrong?*

A: You must tell `imr` where `micod` is running; otherwise `imr` creates its own implementation repository, which is destroyed
upon exit of `imr`. You tell `imr` the location of the implementation repository by using the `-ORBImplRepoAddr` option. For
example:

```
micod -ORBIIOPAddr inet:jade:4242 &
imr -ORBImplRepoAddr inet:jade:4242
```

Q: *I'm new to CORBA. My own MICO application crashes and I cannot find the cause. Please help.*

A: The C++ language mapping is rather complicated and contains lots of pitfalls for CORBA beginners. It is easy to create dangling pointers and memory leaks. Please read Chapter 5 very carefully, especially the sections on strings and operation parameters.

Q: *MICO does not interoperate with ORB X. Help!*

A: This usually indicates that ORB X is not fully CORBA compliant. There are three well-known cases:

1. It basically works, but MICO clients cannot talk to the naming service of ORB X. In this case, ORB X's naming service interfaces do not have the prefix "omg.org" as requested by the CORBA specification. There is no easy way to fix this.

2. It basically works, but MICO clients cannot talk to interfaces inside modules. In this case, ORB X generates wrong repository ids for types inside modules. There is no way to fix this. Some older Orbix versions have this problem.

3. It does not work at all. As of CORBA 2.1, every CORBA request contains information about the character set used by the client, which may confuse ORB X. Give MICO applications the command line option -ORBNoCodeSets to fix this problem (see Section 4.1.1 for details). JacORB 0.9e suffers from this problem.

Glossary

BOA *(Basic Object Adapter)* The BOA is one instance of an object adapter (OA) and serves on the server side as a mediator between the ORB and the object implementation. As its name implies, the BOA offers only primitive services. The BOA's specifications were insufficiently precise and led to a lack in portability in view of vendors' augmentation of the standard. In CORBA version 2.1 the BOA was replaced by the POA.

CG *(Conceptual Graph)* A knowledge representation technique based on a bipartite graph consisting of concepts and relations. Conceptual Graphs allow the representation of arbitrary information in a formalized way. Conceptual graphs are used in MICO for a generic user interface to the DII that allows the invocation of user-definable operations at runtime.

CGI *(Common Gateway Interface)* A specification for transferring information between a WWW server and a CGI program. A CGI program is any program designed to accept and return data that conforms to the CGI specification. The program could be written in any programming language, including C, Perl, Java, or Visual Basic.

CORBA *(Common Object Request Broker Architecture)* An architecture that enables objects to communicate with one another regardless of what programming language they were written in or what operating system they are running on. CORBA was developed by an industry consortium known as the Object Management Group (OMG).

COSS *(Common Object Services Specification)* The COSS defines context-independent services that are often required in application. Services are single-minded modules that bring much of the functionality needed for a truly distributed systems framework. Examples of such services are the naming, event, or security service. MICO offers a variety of services.

DII *(Dynamic Invocation Interface)* The DII is part of the ORB-API on the client side. The client can use it to construct and invoke an operation at runtime. The DII is dynamic in the sense that the operation signature (i.e., its input/output argument types) must not be known at compile time. This is the main difference to IDL stubs, where the interface type is known at compile time.

DSI *(Dynamic Skeleton Interface)* The DSI is part of the ORB-API on the server side. The DSI mirrors the DII functionality on the server side. It is used to deliver an operation invocation to an implementation. As with the DII, the DSI is dynamic in the sense that the operation signature must not be known at compile time.

GIOP *(General Inter-ORB Protocol)* Defines message formats used for communication between ORBs. GIOP is responsible for establishing communication between ORBs. GIOP is part of the interoperability framework whereby applications running on different CORBA implementations are interoperable. GIOP is abstract in the sense that it does not make reference to a specific transport layer.

GNU *(Gnu's Not Unix)* A Unix-compatible software system developed by the Free Software Foundation (FSF). The philosophy behind GNU is to produce software that is non-proprietary. Anyone can download, modify, and redistribute GNU software. The only restriction is that they cannot limit further redistribution. The GNU project was started in 1983 by Richard Stallman at the Massachusetts Institute of Technology.

IDL *(Interface Definition Language)*   The notation used by CORBA to describe object interfaces. This particular notation has distinguished features as it supports subtyping, exception handling, etc. The IDL syntax resembles Java interface and C++ abstract classes declarations. The CORBA standard defines languages mappings, which define rules how to map an IDL specification to a specific programming language.

IIOP *(Internet Inter-ORB Protocol)* IIOP is the instantiation of GIOP using TCP as a transport layer. With respect to GIOP, IIOP only adds transport layer specific details.

IMR *(Implementation Repository)* A database that contains informations on object implementations. This information is typically used by an object adapter during the activation on object implementations.

IOR *(Interoperable Object Reference)* An IOR contains all the information necessary for a client to connect to an object implementation. Among others, the IOR contains a transport layer address as well as an object key of the implementation. The CORBA standard defines a stringified version of an IOR that can be passed to clients by other means (such as email, fax, etc.).

IP *(Internet Protocol)* IP specifies the format of packets, also called datagrams, and the addressing scheme. Most networks combine IP with a higher-level protocol called Transport Control Protocol (TCP), which establishes a virtual connection between a destination and a source.

IR *(Interface Repository)* The IR is a database that maintains IDL specifications of every object interface managed by the ORB. The IR provides an API that allows you to query and modify the interface it manages. The IR provides for the self-describing nature of CORBA objects.

MICO *(Mico Is COrba)* An Open Source implementation of the CORBA standard. The complete source code is placed under the GNU General Public License. MICO pays special attention to CORBA compliance.

OA *(Object Adapter)* CORBA's server side relies on OAs to perform object activation, deactivation, etc. CORBA allows different OAs for different contexts. In some situations special purpose OAs may be used to simplify the processes involved, for example, when communicating with an OODBMS. The POA is the only OA defined by CORBA.

OMG *(Object Management Group)* A consortium with a membership of more than 850 companies. The organization's goal is to provide a common framework for developing applications using object-oriented programming techniques. OMG is responsible for the CORBA specification.

OS *(Open Source)* Open Source promotes software reliability and quality by supporting independant peer review and rapid evolution of source code. Among the many Open Source projects are Linux, Apache, KDE, and, of course, MICO.

ORB *(Object Request Broker)* The ORB is the central piece of the CORBA platform. It serves as an "object bus" connecting different objects. Its main task is the forwarding of operation invocations from client to server objects. The ORB transparently handles networking, name resolution, marshalling, type checking, object activation (see OA), and such.

POA *(Portable Object Adapter)* In essence, the POA tries to augment the BOA with tighter specifications, thereby achieving portability of CORBA applications. POA should peacefully coexist with the BOA as well as with other OAs without disrupting any code.

RM-ODP *(Reference Model for Open Distributed Processing)* The RM-ODP is a joint standard of the International Organization for Standardization (ISO) and the International Telecommunication Union, Telecommunication Standardization Sector (ITU-T). It provides a framework for standardization efforts in the domain of Open Distributed Processing (ODP). The reference model describes an architecture to support distribution, interoperability, and portability.

TCP *(Transmission Control Protocol)* TCP is one of the main protocols in TCP/IP networks. Whereas the IP protocol deals only with packets, TCP enables two hosts to establish a connection and exchange streams of data. TCP guarantees delivery of data and also guarantees that packets will be delivered in the same order in which they were sent.

WWW *(World Wide Web)* A system of Internet servers that support specially formatted documents. The documents are formatted in a language called HTML *(HyperText Markup Language)* that supports links to other documents, as well as graphics, audio, and video files. This means you can jump from one document to another simply by clicking on hot spots. Not all Internet servers are part of the WWW.

Bibliography

[1] M. Henning and S. Vinoski. *Advanced CORBA Programming with C++*. Addison-Wesley Publishing Company, 1999.

[2] ITU.TS Recommendation X.901—ISO/IEC 10746-1: Basic Reference Model of Open Distributed Processing Part 1: Overview and Guide to the Use of the Reference Model, 1994.

[3] ITU.TS Recommendation X.902—ISO/IEC 10746-2: Basic Reference Model of Open Distributed Processing Part 2: Descriptive Model, 1994.

[4] ITU.TS Recommendation X.903—ISO/IEC 10746-3: Basic Reference Model of Open Distributed Processing Part 3: Prescriptive Model, 1994.

[5] ITU.TS Recommendation X.904—ISO/IEC 10746-4: Basic Reference Model of Open Distributed Processing Part 4: Architectural Semantics, 1994.

[6] Object Management Group (OMG), The Common Object Request Broker: Architecture and Specification, Revision 2.3, June 1999.

[7] A. Puder. Introduction to the AI-Trader Project. *www.vsb.informatik.uni-frankfurt.de/projects/aitrader/*, Computer Science Department, University of Frankfurt, 1995.

[8] A. Puder and K. Römer. Using a Metanotation in a CORBA Environment. In *CORBA: Implementation, Use and Evaluation, ECOOP*, Jyväskylä, Finland, June 1997.

[9] J.P. Redlich. *CORBA 2.0—Eine praktische Einführung für C++ und Java*. Addison-Wesley Publishing Company, 1996.

[10] J. Siegel. *CORBA 3: Fundamentals and Programming*. John Wiley & Sons, second edition, 2000.

[11] J.F. Sowa. *Conceptual Structures, Information Processing, Mind and Machine*. Addison-Wesley Publishing Company, 1984.

[12] A. Tanenbaum and A. Woodhull. *Operating Systems: Design and Implementation*. Prentice/Hall International, second edition, 1997.

Index

Morgan Kaufmann Publishers and dpunkt.verlag MICO End User License Agreement

This is a contract. By using this product you accept all the terms and conditions of this agreement. This Morgan Kaufmann Publishers and dpunkt.verlag (collectively "the Publisher") End User License Agreement accompanies the MICO compiled binaries ("Object Code") and the MICO Source Code on the CD (collectively the "Software"), and the related explanatory materials (the "Publication," collectively "the Product"). Please read this Agreement carefully. If you do not agree to these terms, do not use this Product. Return it with all accompanying items within 30 days to the Publisher for a full refund of the purchase price.

Use of the Product Publication and Object Code

No part of this Publication or the MICO Object Code may be reproduced, stored in a retrieval system, or transmitted in any form or by any means: electronic, mechanical, photocopying, recording, or otherwise, without the prior, written permission of the Publisher.

Use of the Product Source Code

The MICO Source Code is published under the GNU General Public License, as described in Chapter 9 of the Publication. You agree to the terms of this license.

Limited Warranty

The Publisher warrants the media on which the software is furnished to be free from defects in materials and workmanship under normal use for 30 days from the date that you obtain the Product. The warranty set forth above is the exclusive warranty pertaining to the Product, and the Publisher disclaims all other warranties, express or implied, including, but not limited to, implied warranties of merchantability and fitness for a particular purpose, even if the Publisher has been advised of the possibility of such purpose. Some jurisdictions do not allow limitations on an implied warranty's duration, therefore the above limitations may not apply to you.

Limitation of Liability

Your exclusive remedy for breach of this warranty will be the repair or replacement of the Product at no charge to you or the refund of the applicable purchase price paid upon the return of the Product, as determined by the Publisher in its discretion. In no event will the Publisher, and its directors, officers, employees, and agents, or anyone else who has been involved in the creation, production, or delivery of this software be liable for indirect, special, consequential, or exemplary damages, including, without limitation, for lost profits, business interruption, lost or damaged data, or loss of goodwill, even if the Publisher or an authorized dealer or distributor or supplier has been advised of the possibility of such damages. Some jurisdictions do not allow the exclusion or limitation of indirect, special, consequential, or exemplary damages or the limitation of liability to specified amounts, therefore the above limitations or exclusions may not apply to you.